Attitude of Sun

Attitude of Sun

by Bruce B. Wilmer

Published by:

Winding Brook Press

P. O. Box 7, Burnsville, NC 28714

This book is a compilation of new poems
plus 41 poems previously copyrighted by the author
in his books of poetry, FEELINGS; LOVE POEMS; BELIEVE IN
YOURSELF: POEMS OF PURPOSE; TIME CRIES: A POET'S
RESPONSE TO 9/11/01; POEMS TO CARRY WITH YOU ON
LIFE'S JOURNEY: INSPIRATION AND ENCOURAGEMENT FOR
EVERY NEW BEGINNING; and POEMS FOR THE ONE I LOVE.

Cover photo at the summit of Mt. LeConte by Bruce B. Wilmer
Author photo by Sydney Wilmer
Cover design by Bruce and Sydney Wilmer
Invaluable editing and suggestions by Sydney Wilmer
Thanks to Jeremy and Kristen for all their helpful input.

https://www.brucebwilmer.com

ISBN: 978-1-57158-001-6

For Sydney,
who brought
rays of sunshine
into my life

INTRODUCTION

I grew up watching my artist parents in a multitude of settings with their paints, brushes and easels as they observed and celebrated life and the world around them through the colorful paintings and sketches they created. They also crafted pictures of life and their surroundings through words and poetry. They relished the creative life in all its forms and inspired creativity in me. The poems in ATTITUDE OF SUN are sketches and celebrations of some of the details of my own life and the natural world and communities I have known. I focus on the many wonders and unique and sometimes poignant details of each. I hope my poetic descriptions of scenes and settings will liberate a flow of thoughts and memories in you, the reader, as I 'pay forward' my gratitude for other poetic voices reaching across time to ease the solitude of our human condition.

The radiant sun in ATTITUDE OF SUN drives our seasons and illuminates our days, predictably rising and setting, often with an amazing array of colors. As a metaphor for archetypal beginnings and endings, it bathes us at times in both joy and sadness. This book covers that broad spectrum of human emotions and sometimes shifts to wider concerns about the planet and the travails of its people.

The poems are arranged alphabetically, for lack of a better organizing principle, so suburban and mountain themes are intermingled, meandering from populous North to rural South and back. They are heartfelt, empathetic, with occasional wry overtones, and tied to a feeling of respect and dignity for all creatures and the natural habitat we share as we coexist and traverse the seasons together on this fragile speck of dust in our vast universe.

—Bruce B. Wilmer
Western NC (2019)

CONTENTS

Unexpected moments
Can our memories endow.
Tomorrow finds its riches in
The commonplace of now.

from Present Perfect (page 225)

Attitude of Sun

A DAY WITH SUN

A day with sun
   Erases bleak thoughts,
      Bakes out shadows,
         Burns away negatives.
In the warming rays,
   We reach out
      From deep caverns of thought
         To rediscover ourselves.
We lift up our heads
   To survey life,
      To feel the vibrant power
         Of the universe,
To become one
   With the coursing, throbbing mass
      Called nature.

On such days,
   We're part of the whole,
      Existing as a true detail of being,
         Organically complete and fulfilled,
Drinking the oxygen of the moment,
   Indulging in the abundance of time,
      Ripe with moment,
         Rare with self.

➤

Clouds desist
    As night settles in
    And we relax
        In past day's potential,
Reality placed
    In colorful wrapping
      And left unopened
        As time dissolves
And we glide away,
    Grateful for the gift of a day
    Filled with sun.

ACCUMULATION

The hush of night
   Fell over cotton soft snow
      As wind quietly sculpted
        And rounded all edges.

A full day spent
   Blanketed my thoughts with fatigue,
      Subduing all details,
        Softening the noises of memory.

In the warmth of the moment
   I lay in bed
      Embracing my pillow,

Conforming to the surface,
   Silently sculpting myself
      To the night,

Covers glancing over me,
   Letting me become invisible
      To the day...
        And myself.

ALL I HAD WAS THE WARM

As your breath deepened
    Into nothing,
The expected half-rise of your chest
    Never fulfilled,
Life abated
    And slipped away
        Unpretentiously
           Into perpetual pause.
Your heart that pulsed existence
    For 75 years
        Now stood still.

The distance between
    The last beat
        And the first silence,
While straining for significance,
    Was so soft and natural
        That one perceived no line
But merely an unmarked border
    Between life and death
        That somehow redistributed
        Your spirit
And transmuted your energy
    Through and out of
        The material world.

When breath's motion stopped,
    The pump of life ceased its vigil,
        And blood gave up
        Its role of renewal,

Your forehead proclaimed
     That life had once been here,
And I held your warmth in
     With my hand pressed caringly
          To your now relaxed furrows,
Returning the love
     That had once helped me
          Through trial and change.

For these waning moments,
     All I had was the warm.

As your life bled
     Into the ages,
I drew another gust
     Of your spirit
          Into my heart,
Knowing that time would
     Enrich me still further
As if my hand
     Could remain on your forehead
          Touching the warmth
               Of your vibrant life
                    Forever.

ALONE

Alone in the world,
   Facing it all
      In a bare footnote
         To time,

Watching beauty and aridness,
   Of spirit and place,
      Unfold and unravel,

Carrying being
   Through heartfelt seasons
      On trodden paths
         To human endings,

Organic and full,
   Viewing that final dust
      With tragic reserve,

Alone in the world,
   Alone in thought,
      Alone in mortal wondering,

Alone in life,
   Save for you,

But you are a part of me
   And we move and exist
      In all things,
         In all ways,
            As one,

Time treating us as one,
Love bonding us as one,
Eternity holding
One tear for us both.

AN HOUR TO ASHEVILLE

Our usual 45 minute drive to Asheville
    Stretches to an hour,
As the February sun
    Invigorates an army of earth movers—
Shaving, shaping and expanding
    The Route 19 corridor
        To four lanes.

Bronzed flagmen,
    Bundled against crisp air,
        Retard our journey,
Letting yellow giants
    Cross traffic
        To dispense their earthen cargo
            As others return for more.

Colossal dozers stroke
    Massive hillsides lower
        Toward payloader buckets
            Which feed the lined up trucks
Casually arrayed in a
    Tonka Toy extravaganza.

Delays are repeated along the journey
    As other turns are straightened,
        Depressions filled in,
            Drainage enabled;
And houses or businesses
    In the designated pathway
        Dutifully yield front yards, parking, acreage—
            Or whole structures—
                To the swallowing roadbed.

Churches along the route,
Affirm their ties
With the Almighty
(And accommodating politicians),
Being rather miraculously pardoned
By state surveyors
Who leave them untouched
By the relentless
Purveyors of progress.

Granite outcroppings and stately overlooks,
Once nearly impervious to time,
Yield to dynamite assaults
And ruthless rock crushers
Redistributing their might
Into invisible road base.

Forests disappear
With chainsaw logic—
Loud-throated chippers
Reducing canopied habitats
Into vast piles of organic debris,
Loggers dispatching straight growth timber
To sawmill yards
For conversion
Into house lumber.

Most don't ask, but certainly must know,
Where squirrels, turtles, snakes,
Nesting birds, and a host of
Small forest creatures end up,

➤

Brutally lost to expansive views
     And hastened travel,
Callously consumed
     In the way of progress.

Soon we will cut our time to Asheville
     By four or five minutes
And won't have to quell impatience
     Behind an unhurried farmer
          In his exhaust-belching pickup.

We will get to where we are going
     That much sooner,
          Without the need to slow
               For untamed bends
                    In the narrow country road
Or wonder if a deer
     Might suddenly show up
          On a tree-lined shoulder
               To remind us
                    Of minor mysteries and marvels
Crafted by an Almighty
     Not always amenable to
          The ideas and wishes of
               Planners and politicians.

ANOTHER REQUIEM

Wren's mighty solo
    Trumpeted from deck post
      Again and again
        In quarter turns
          Declares end of day.
With upraised beak
    And distended throat,
Half-pint performer
    Makes a clear statement about
    The world of our deck,
      Seized now as stage.

Inside, a Brahms chorus
    Fills living room speakers
      With heavenly song,
Yet hardly rivals upstart wren
    Singing with feeling
      Beyond kitchen window.

As nature's message
    Competes with cathedral sounds
      Wrung from living room speakers,
We notice wren's concluding,
    And untimely,
      Lift-off
        Into our dense planter of ferns.

➤

Jarred from reverie,
　　We sense that choosy visitor
　　　And her already hidden mate
　　　　Have just ratified their choice
Of the swinging planter
　　For their next brood,
　　　As they shimmy the vegetation
　　　　With excitement.

These are likely the same two
　　Whose ill-fated last brood
　　　Of fledgling fliers
Was launched not long ago
　　From a neighbor's planter
　　　Into the unexpected path
　　　　Of her lovable old dog,
Stirring his birder instincts
　　And giving today's outdoor requiem
　　　By this impassioned wren
　　　　A truly authentic ring.

APPETITE FOR LIFE

Autumn swallows
  The hillside
And washes its color
  Away.

Indoor plants
  Under windows
Cling to an island
  Of warm.

Winter focuses life
  In small places,
Rationing color,
  Harboring hope.

Then spring dances in
  And eagerly
Jars life from
  Earth's memory,

Renewing the hillside,
  Refreshing nature's miracles—
Once dwindled
  To a few potted plants

Hopefully placed
  Beneath sunny windows
In an island
  Of warm.

APRIL MOOD

A magnificent night—
    The dark is panting;
Evening swallows
    All the stars.

Air is wet
    Without a droplet.
Wind with every
    Treetop spars.

Sky is writhing;
    Moon is drowning;
Pink is oozing
    From the clouds.

Night attempts
    To wrap the heavens
In its gray and
    Dismal shrouds.

All the trees
    In mixed confusion
Fret this loss of
    Starlit sky.

Dreams will soon
    Ascend the moment,
Left in swirling seas
    To fly.

APRIL SNOW

The splendor of
    An April day
With balmy mood
    And winds at play

Could not foresee
    The shock in store
For buds and blooms
    With one day more.

I thought I knew
    What April was
With tulips and
    Forsythias,

But on the morrow
    I would rise
With gusting snow
    Before my eyes.

The chill undid
    Magnolia pink,
Disarmed its petals
    In a wink.

The insects that
    In clusters flew
Were stilled in a
    Climactic coup.

➤

The robins rapt
  Before the freeze
Now trudged in snow
  Up to their knees.

And though the energy
  Of spring
Fell hard in winter's
  Final fling,

I saw within
  This crystal cold
Forsythia's
  Insistent gold

And knew, though frigid
  Winds did dance,
New life would have
  A second chance;

And snows that covered
  April's show
Would roll up winter's jest
  And go.

ATTITUDE OF SUN

I stepped into a new day
    With an attitude of sun.
I heard no more the silence,
    For the music had begun.

The chorus was astounding—
    Many colors, many tunes.
It seemed that early Aprils
    Could out-sing the later Junes.

Enthusiasm tinted spring—
    I felt the season start.
With not one leaf to trill about,
    The birds expressed their heart.

The day was damp and chill with rain
    That sputtered now and then;
But sun had risen in my soul,
    For spring was once again.

BAT BALLET

Four bats—above, about, beyond and by—
    Swooping, mixing,
        Emphatically involved
            In the ballet of bugs,

Fluttering acrobats,
    Punctuating black
        Against the twilit sky,
Culling the air
    Of unwary insects,

Paired and parted,
    Sensuous and independent,
All over, everywhere,
    Exiting without a trace,
        Then back again,

Harbingers of night,
    Open-mouthed and eager,
        Lethal to those in their path,
Yet somehow benign and comforting
    In their agile choreography,
In their amazing grace
    And lofty finality
        When the curtain of their act
        Invisibly closes,

Pointing with their past
    To a possible tomorrow,
        At this same time,
When their darting mystery
    Will again intrigue the heavens.

BETTER VIEW

They moved their blankets
    Closer to the stage,
The better to see
    The performers,
The better for us
    To see them perform.

As the wind quintet,
    Alternating with poets,
        Played and recited
            Their night's fare,
The couple's probing fish lips
    Planted their random love
        Upon each other's
            Necks and above.

As the play unfolded,
    Growing in intensity,
        Their play unfolded,
            Growing in intensity.

The focus on-stage
    Was only matched
        By their distraction
        Off.

➢

19

I'm not sure which show,
    Intended or impromptu,
        Caught my attention more,
Or what form of love,
    So intoxicated with itself,
Could convert a two-hour evening
    Of music and poetry
Into a steamy display
    Of exhibitionism,
        As two hungry mouths
            Obsessively explored each other
            On a hillside of hundreds.

BETWEEN SHADOWS

Meeting matter,
Resolving in time,
Focusing in flesh,
I am here,
Caught in the moment,
Drenched in warm molecules,
Suspended between shadows.

I look for a path
From one shadow
To the next,
Attempting to lay
Joy and purpose
Over foreboding.

I am only partially
Successful
As the path behind me
Elongates
And that ahead
Contracts

And I alternately
Cherish
And bewail
The whole progression
Of needless,
Spectacular,
Callous and unremitting
Steps through time.

BILLOW

Sail, parachute,
    Hot air balloon,
Holiday Santa or snowman,
    Engorged with artificial
        Updraft.

So billows my spirit
    Against collapse
        With puffs of imagination,
Propelling me forward, slowing my fall,
    Lifting me up, proclaiming me—
Countering descent, decline,
    Deflation.

How strong the construct must be
    For porting the spirit gently
        On its way,
As fantasies and
    Fascinations
        Fill their lofting role
In the gusty ascents
    And brazen stands
        That are life.

BOLEN'S CREEK

Invigorated by sweat
    And warm exhaustion,
We race the waning light
    On the heavy heels of descent.

We hear the approach
    Of the brook we passed
        Hours before,
Having resisted its curious chatter
    And the interesting spur
        In the trail
            Leading to it.

Now, spent physically
    And distanced
        From the summit,
We are drawn in
    By the calming sound of
        Water on rocks
And the cold, fresh mystery
    Of a dark pool,
Modestly hidden
    In the forest clearing.

We shed hiking boots and socks
    And chill our feet
        And tender sore ankles
           In the sparkling flow.

➤

You watch as I then pile
　　My remaining sweaty clothes
　　　　On a rock
And refresh my exposed skin
　　In the drying air.

I take my accumulated warmth
　　Into the pool's brisk, dark rinse
　　　　And stroke my saline-slick pores clean,
　　　　　　Immersing up to my neck.

You watch this chill exercise,
　　Glancing now and again toward
　　　　Our empty fragment of trail—
　　　　　　Just in case—
As I then leave the invigorating liquid
　　And stand again to air and pat dry
　　　　In the light evening breeze.

I welcome your familiar gaze,
　　Yet wish your observing form—
　　　　Shuddering at the frigid, sunless waters—
Could shed your concerns,
　　And all else,
　　　　Adding your own striking view
　　　　　　To the summits already achieved.

BOSTON NIGHT

Street lights entertain
    Through blinds
As leaf hands pluck silently
    At wall-shadowed harp strings.

Thus does early winter
    Gust its surreal
        Apology
For snow and ice
    Shaken onto cars below
        On Halloween eve.

Whatever lures the next day's
    Spooks and goblins,
This high-spirited haunt
    In the restless morning dark
Is surely the warm-up
    For ice floes of ghouls and parents
Who will soon drift
    Up and down sidewalks
        And jar loose another shiver
          Of wintry amazement.

BOX TURTLES

Box turtles lumber into sight
   In deep summer,
      Venturing out from
         Their discreet forest hideaways.

Lured to scarce rain puddles
   For luxuriant mud baths
      Or warm fields for incubating eggs
         Or social interactions,
They cross our lives unexpectedly,
   Hardly aware of our competition
      For their ancestral habitat,
         And calmly asserting their prior claim.

We stare at each other and coexist,
   Though at times we, the bigger,
      May lift them up
         Out of harm's way,
Eliciting a tight clamshell response
   Or a cautious peek at our intruding form,
      Their head and legs halfway in.

As we try to anticipate their destination,
   Advancing them on their journey,
      A concern we repeat through the years,
There is hopefully a mutual feeling
   Of childlike wonder and respect
And a sense that though we are
   An occasional impediment to their progress,
      We are harmless in their eyes.

BREATHLESS NIGHT

On a breathless,
    Window-open night,
Noiseless, but for the usual
    Night chattering,

I lie in a harmony
    Of inside air,
Inhaling the respectful
    Outside mild.

Such stillness and equilibrium
    Fill a moment
When one season lingers
    And another has yet to begin.

I feel the sensory equivalent
    Of peace,
The perceptual place
    Of balance.

In this relaxation
    Of the seasons,
It's hard to mobilize thought,
    Entertain focus.

I float on my back,
    Trawling for dreams
In the posh quiet of a concept
    Suspended in mid-air.

BREEZY RIDER

Pelican prowls the breezes,
    Sentry to underlying channel,
Ungainly diver for slivers
    Of sustenance—
Those silver-scaled tidbits
    Teasing the surface
        In deadly pursuit
            Of their own prey.

Pelican sights along sabered bill
    The possibilities of a ripple,
Plans the plunge,
    Designs an exclamation point
        As the end to a lofty hunt.

Pelican thoughtfully
    Plodding the currents
        Now immerses
            In sudden athletics.

Plumb-lining from high to low,
    This feathered missile
        Breaks the near-glass surface
        Without slowing
And spears the unlucky ripple,
    Downing its shadowy presence
        In one gulp.

Returning to the surface,
Bobbing up to rearrange
Respectability,
The stately pelican
Politely sheds
Any hint of water
And shrugs into
A momentary smile,
Taking a tranquil breaktime
On the water.

A bit hard to relax, however,
When other tasty morsels
Ride the ripples,
And hunger prods the hunter.

Ponderous pelican
Thus lifts off
To start again
His forever-quest
For one more aerobatic,
Face crashing,
Ration of enrichment...
And bliss.

BUMBLEBEE

Bumblebee in grasp of death,
    Bumblebee with talons tight,
Nursing nectar 'til the end
    Without the will to flee in flight.

Bumblebee in ecstasy
    As raucous rotors near,
Clinging to the very last
    Without a trace of fear.

Bumblebee embracing life,
    You have no need to fly;
Bumblebee, in pure devotion
    You may shortly die.

Bumblebee, at least you do not
    Fight the fates and fear them;
But rotors are the risks of life
    And I, alone, must hear them.

BURNSVILLE TOWN SQUARE:
4TH OF JULY WEEKEND

Solemn words and rituals
And a young lady's heart-rending
National Anthem
Open the 4th of July fair,
As nearby church chimes compete.

Throughout the day,
Musicians on stage
Amplify their diverse styles
For the scattered crowd.

Young dancers pound the holiday stage
With emphatic rhythms.
Spirited children roll over and over
On the cushiony grass
And prance the green corridors
Between folding chairs
In joyful display.

Face painters transform other children
Patient enough to wait in line
Into something bright and silly.
Artists and craftsmen magnet themselves
To passersby
From their canvas booths
Crammed with creations.

➤

Sizzling, smoking barbecue tents
   Summon mid-afternoon appetites
      To juicy snacks
         Heaped with fixin's.
Other tents tempt with frosty root beers
And fruit smoothies.

Rain hides in the clouds
   But soon lets go and harvests
      A wildflower field of umbrellas.
During the shower, the dulcimer player
   Charms us with her melodious mix
      And then poignantly concludes with,
         "When you and I were young, Maggie,"
A piece our daughter, not long before,
   Had brought to life in piano and song
      While exploring my late mother's
         Tattered box of sheet music.

The tune pierces my heart with recall,
   As memory leaps to my mother's lithe hands
      Dancing over familiar keys
         In a far-off living room.

Sitting there in the town square,
   I roam time's vault of small moments,
      Painfully aware how priceless they turn
         With each passing season.

I look at you
    In the evolving light,
Our forms pressed close
    On the low circular wall,
My thoughts unconsciously scanning
    Our decades together,
Unable to keep from humming once again,
    Long after the dulcimer has left the stage,
    "When you and I were young."

BUTTERFLY CITY

Tall, exultant echinacea
    Near your friend, majestic lily,
Blend your striking pinks together,
    Lure your fliers willy nilly.

Lily, cast your sweet aroma
    From your bed seductively.
Echinacea, add your essence—
    Spread your scent instructively.

Draw the bees and insects closer;
    Lure their varied shapes and sizes.
Share your nectar with all comers—
    Dole abundance, deal your prizes.

Let your beauty be a magnet,
    For those beauties flying by.
Lift your faces proudly upward—
    Tell the swallowtails, "Come nigh."

Bid them into your hearts softly.
    Let them light and float around.
Let them join this buzzing city,
    Tap your gifts without a sound.

Sights and scents intoxicate them,
    Launch them into dances stunning.
Delving deep, they stand aflutter,
    Intimate with blossoms sunning.

Butterflies and moths and more
   Pursue the joys a day affords.
On your petals, probing, searching,
   They extract your sweet rewards,

In this city of surprises,
   Source of high exhilaration,
Nature soon will end the frolic,
   Still this frantic celebration.

Time will tick away abundance;
   Players will rejoin the soil.
Days organic will conclude
   This brash display of colors royal.

CAMERA OF MY MIND

Little Abyssinian,
  Posing on the sill,
Locked in meditation,
  Like a silent daffodil,

Facing our hibiscus
  With its open orange flowers,
You imbue our morning view
  With tranquilizing powers.

Now I see these blossoms
  Nearly withered in their place
And miss the mood of sun
  And look of peace upon your face.

But there are soothing images,
  Impressions that I find,
In moments of reflection
  In the camera of my mind.

And when those scant suggestions
  Of a faded past occur,
I view a proud hibiscus
  With an audience of fur.

CARDINAL DELIGHT

Always standing out in color,
    Capturing attention smartly,
Drawing gazes to your redness,
    While your mate is hidden partly.

You're a contrast to the seasons,
    With their green and gold and white.
You're a ruddy wisp of nature,
    Brazenly reflecting light.

Many creatures blend in earthy tones
    And hide their presence.
You are there to advertise
    Your brash and fiery essence.

There is nothing like your blaze
    For visual surprises.
Your arrival on a branch
    Alerts and energizes.

Nature greets us everywhere,
    Repeating its grand story;
But when your crimson form appears,
    We're struck with all its glory.

CARDINAL OFFENSE

Standing on deck railing,
     Peering crossly at yourself
          In polished glass,
Posturing at the very
     Threat of you
          Mirrored back
               From dinette window,
You defend your turf,
     Uphold your honor,
          Protect your mate.

You twist your head,
     Lower your stance,
          Bob from side to side,
Quarrel with that
     Brazen red likeness
Challenging you sternly
     With equal bounce and brass.

You attack the window
     Several times,
          Pecking at that defiant
               Red phantom,
Hoping to make your point,
     Expel this interloper,
          Quell his hubris.

With strikes mercilessly repeated,
    Lessons firmly told,
You dip and glide away
    To nearby pine branch,
Victorious warrior
    Calmly surveying
        The site of the incursion,
Confidently assaying
    Your antagonist's
        Hasty departure.

With such courageous antics,
    Your mate will most certainly
        Honor and protect
            Your feathered nobility
Should another challenge arise
    In the form of
        A buff, ruddy-edged female,
Drawn to your charisma
    And brash bird brain activism;
And she will undoubtedly respond
    With equal verve
        Should the other dare to commit
        That same cardinal offense.

CAT ON BED

I'm lying here with lump of fur,
    A round of raw potential purr,
Compressed against my crowded toes—
    Asleep, I meet a stretch that grows.

The press of paw I must ignore
    When padded feet my peaks explore.
A cool, wet nose approaches mine.
    This heavy breath has one design—

To get me in the proper mood
    To rouse myself to serve some food.
That done, I've no more dreams to reap,
    Yet purry pal returns to sleep;

And while I stare upon the ceiling,
    A plump indent of fur I'm feeling—
A peaceful shape that fussed till fed
    On what I thought was my own bed.

And though it seems a place to sleep,
    I must the right perspective keep—
I'm servant to a feline that
    Behaves like an aristo-cat.

CATCHING THE WIND

Crows catch the wind
    And throw themselves to and fro
      In the urgent air of morning.
There is no end to their play
    As they fill the wide screen of sky
      With black-dart daring
        And brazen choreography.

Goaded by group,
    Bursting with day's euphoria,
They launch themselves
    Into problematic sky,
      Drawn by racing clouds
        Advancing an upward sun.

With frantic energy and near grace,
    They depart as they arrived,
      In competing chaos,
        Maneuvering mightily
In dips and swings,
    With peril and pride,
      Gallivanting the gusts,
Saluting, defying the icy bleakness
    With uproarious aplomb
      And seemingly endless strength of wing
        And mid-winter optimism.

CHILD, PAUSE A WHILE

Child, pause a while;
   Stem your hurried pace;
And in life's book
   Just let me mark this place.

Your fleeting journey
   Scarce allows delay.
Your hopes and dreams
   Press on in their own way.

So cherished are the moments
   Rushing by
That I can only seize
   The hour and sigh.

Had I but known how fast
   You'd skim each stage,
I would have marked your book
   At every page.

CHOREOGRAPHY

Not just surface ripples or waves,
But myriad minuets
Spinning circles on glass
Enhanced by grey sky.

Not bleak,
This dark impromptu dancing
And unplanned partying
Of breezes on water
Tips my wonder,
Electrifies the moment
With soft swirling textures.

These breaths of wind,
In feathery foreplay,
Cast quiet phrases
Over harbor surfaces,
Locking me into the moment.

I am mesmerized by motion,
Awed by patterns of peace.

As rain sprinkles its first,
Erasing these spirits
Of dance,
I think,
How subtle nature is
In stirring
The surface of my dreams.

CLOUDLAND TRAIL

We track the sun along the trail—
    Our winter thoughts tucked far away;
But as we reach the churning summit,
    Racing clouds devour day.

Angry winds whip hair and face
    And burn the cold into our skin.
Nature that has been so still
    Expresses passions through the din.

We approach the edge of all
    And carefully look down.
We see a frothing alchemy
    In which a soul could drown.

We feel the might around us
    Telling us to hold on tight.
We linger in that moment,
    At the limits of our sight.

The clouds are all about us
    In a hurry to get by.
We have a sense of how the heights
    Would feel if we could fly.

We back off from this land of angels
    With a gasp and awe.
We freeze in dreams the mystery
    Of nature in the raw.

And when such peaks in untamed moments
    Lose their caring sun,
We see how clouds and restless winds
    Can dash the peace and run.

CLOUDY VIEW

Fog undoes morning,
    Cancels the sunrise,
Paints the blue sky pale,
    And leaves darkened, drab
        Trees in the foreground.

More distant trees
    Breathe in and out
        Of reality,
Unsure of their hold
    On the day.

The mountains waive their stature,
    Relinquish their dominance
        Over the landscape
And forgo their luminous answer
    To the rising sun.

The day's white amnesia
    Masks all details
        In tantalizing vagueness,
Lingering so long
    Even the birds are sobered
        By its message.

CLUMP OF FLOWERS

On a roadside rife with brush,
  I saw a clump of yellow flowers.
Caring hands some years before
  Had buried bulbs imbued with powers.

As I now drive past the colors
  Left in gardens no more groomed,
I observe the faith required
  To yield all that's newly bloomed.

I accept the kindly greeting
  From a schemer in the past
When I view this clump of flowers
  Left with love and meant to last.

COEXISTENCE

Daylight draws me
   To the dinette table
      And its feast of laptop news,
As a hungry rabbit—
   Framed by our window—
      Grazes our salad of hillside.

As I migrate screen to screen,
   Tawny vegetarian
      Migrates plant to plant,
Razors the tallest blades,
   Reeling them in
      To their tender tops,
         Which vanish spaghetti-like.

My gaze outward
   Prompts an occasional
      Return stare.
But, silent and scentless,
   I am as invisible
      As a bird poking its ration
         Of worms and insects.

How systematically
   I cull my field
      Of news articles:
How diligently
   The foraging hare
      Prunes our hillside.

We exist in balance—
   Unthreatening,
      Remote to each other's senses—
A truce easily snuffed
   Should incisive rodent appetite
      Shift its attention
         To my endangered azalea
            At the top of the hill,
Causing me to shed my equanimity,
   Unlatch and raise my window,
      Bellow harsh threats
         And unkind words,
And, for the moment at least,
   Bash any suggestion
      Of civility or coexistence.

COMMUNITY POOL IN WINTER

Despite the cold, forbidding dark—
    All vestiges of summer gone—
A cool, refreshing cache of plenty
    Throws its cheery light till dawn.

Coca Cola is the message;
    Coca Cola bellows out;
Coca Cola's winning sparkle
    Is the fizz it's all about.

All is drab and lost to night,
    A bleak motif of gray,
Except the red and white machine
    With zesty things to say.

Frosty, icy and inviting—
    Partying around the clock—
Trying to awaken thirst,
    To stir and influence the flock.

All around, the world is sleeping—
    People nestled in their beds.
For the stragglers chancing by,
    This soft drink beacon turns their heads.

This cool fluorescent scene may strike them
    Strange in winter's air;
But not too far away it's likely
    Pepsi beams its truth somewhere.

These sentinels keep up their pitch
    When frigid winds are blowing.
Though summer is still months away,
    Their frozen hearts keep glowing.

COUNTRY GRAVEYARD

Granite outcroppings
    Oversee granite shapes
        Fenced in a gated enclosure.
Time's casual relics above,
    Piercing the grass slope,
        Gather century's soil
            And watch the human geometry
           Accumulate below.

The chiseled, named stones,
    Set carefully on lower hillside,
        Harbor fragile memories,
Soon lost to life
    When life can no more
        Color in the caring inscriptions.

In time, this disciplined granite
    Becomes just another outcropping
        Like those sculpted above
           With geologic patience.

COUNTRY ROAD

Rounding one bend,
   I approach another
With its overlooking pasture
   And radiant spectacle of
     Three magnificent
      Tan horses.

Facing the sunset,
   Tails astir,
Muscles defined
   In proud self-support,

These taut structures
   Swipe their tawny sides
     Dramatically,
Heads and necks swinging erect
   After bending to the moist grass.

In a flash, the history of
   Discovery, conquest and pioneering
Radiates from their intense
   Dignity and self-possession.

I continue past them
   As I negotiate the S-turn
     At reduced speed,
And my mind slows
   To let a memorable image
Majestically conclude
   An otherwise
     Commonplace day.

COZY CONFERENCE

He took his father's hand
  And, securely light-footed,
    Walked two steps to his dad's one
    Until reaching dock's end,
Where each absorbed
  The other's awe
    And, sitting cross-legged,
      Divulged their soft amazement
     At the lapping waters
      Colored by close of day.

Caught up in their spell
  And seeing my own past
   In their present,
I envied their
  Closely-held surprise,
   Their secret musings,
     Nonsensical nothings.

As observer
  Relaxing high-up
   On distant deck,
I regretted the finish
  Of their cozy conference,
As the sun dipped out of sight,
  The breeze sharpened its kiss,
   Their shapes retreated,
    And the time for recall
     Slipped away.

CROW FEET

Skating our metallic roof,
   They pelt our ears
      With chalkboard squeaks
         And grating squabbles,
Spewing news
   And prating views
      With effusive caws
         In jabbering chorus.

I track their silly rantings
   From one end of the roof
      To the other,
Unable to decide
   If they are just gabbing gossips
      Or a sage representative body.

My mind casually shifts
   To the endless talk
      Of our own elected officials—
Each with a following,
   Each with a leader,
      Each with a blustery take on things—
Spewing verbiage, aiming points,
   Jabbing the opposition,
      Strutting the stage,
         Milking the moment.

➤

I link crows and politicians
Cozily together in the same thought,
Noting the noisy drama
And proud posturing of both,
Unable to credit the latter, however,
With the extenuating feral innocence
Or wild candor
Of the former.

DAFFODILS

The daffodils impatiently
    Poke up ahead of grass.
They spike the forest edges,
    Launch their luscious greens en masse.

The drabness of the hillside
    Meets the dullness of the wood
Until these verdant signs of hope
    Regale the neighborhood.

It's not the time for mowing grass
    Or making gardens grow.
It's only time for savoring
    This unexpected show.

Yellow blossoms follow soon
    And bellow out with force
A farewell message to the cold
    As winter runs its course.

Trumpets proudly blow away
    The season without guilt.
The earliest are fated first
    To bend their heads and wilt.

Later blooms then tip away
    And focus on the earth
And melt into the green that formed
    The color of their birth.   ➤

These hardy remnants celebrate
   A prelude that is past,
Their yellow trumpets having stirred
   A vibrant springtime cast;

And as the pulse of life increases,
   Working toward its goal,
These daffodils, the harbingers,
   Have played a vital role.

DAY IS DONE

Day is done—
    The light has passed.
The night rolls in,
    Its presence vast.

I'm lost in stillness,
    Quiet thought.
I scan the meanings
    Day has taught.

I try to milk
    This moment's peace,
Reluctant to let go,
    Release.

But then my grasp
    Begins to slip.
My night awareness
    Sheds its grip.

I drift away
    In random bliss
To nurse the night's
    Warm nothingness.

DAY OF NIGHT

The deck is lit
  With moonlight,
The day of night
  Presiding.

We face our windowed doors
  From bed,
In quilted comfort
  Hiding.

We listen to the
  Noises
As the chilly winds
  Rush by.

We fit together,
  Trading warmth,
As front to back
  We lie.

I ride my hand
  Around your form,
As sight and sound
  And feel

Collaborate
  In harmony
The wintry cold
  To heal.

DEATH DANCE

Tautly hung
   In morning sun
      Outside dinette window,
A depleted web
   With scattered insect relics
      Responds to a soft suggestion of wind.

What was once an intricate array
   Of concentric weavings
Is now a skeleton
   Of rugged suspensory elements
      Targeting a center stage
Where the web's meticulous craftsman—
   Motionless predator—
      Once lay in wait.

This weathered masterwork
   Recalls evening spectacles
      Of winged curiosity-seekers
Drawn into careless death dances
   By nocturnal lighting.

The drama of this occasional harvest
   Usually escaped notice;
But by morning,
   An array of tightly bound remains
      Attested to nighttime
         Industry and determination.

➤

Now, with the web's efficient
　　Crosshatching gone,
Unconsumed gnats and feasts
　　And leftover legs and limbs
　　　Sway insecurely
　　　　In the tattered filament,
Marking the clock's rude advance,
　　The cycle complete,
　　　The vigilance ended.

DECISIONS OF VALUE

Clay smile
    From wry old man
      On oval print
        Stabs through glass
          Into the subconscious.

On the wall near her bookcase
    It quietly teased
      The senses,
        Tickling funny bones,
        Parodying death.

When the liquidator
    Cleared the contents out
      For a flat $500,
Certain things of no value
    Stayed behind,
      Decidedly the objects
        Of sentiment...
          Or incineration.

The old man,
    Placed in our car,
      Then in an upstairs hall,
Having survived the liquidator's
    Frugal bid,
      The incinerator's
        Burning indifference,

➤

Is now here,
　　Beaming out from our wall
　　　　(Or, in time, maybe stacked
　　　　　　In a dusty closet corner)
Till some distant party
　　Happens to connect again
　　　　With the enigmatic good will
　　　　Of this stony gaze,

Giving it further life
　　In the perceptions,
　　　　Where no concern is paid
　　　　　For stark appraisals
　　　　　　Of 'no value'
And where the heart commands
　　All decisions
　　　　Of real value.

DEER RUN

Diverting and delaying our return
    Along the usual route,
We stand at river's edge,
    Off a back road,
To watch the calm wide flow
    Funnel into soft washboard rapids.

As the rain-healthy river
    Threads the treed margins
        Of fallow farmlands,
We shift our glance
    To a line of six tiptoeing deer
        On the opposite bank
            Fixated on their crossing point.

The leader unexpectedly
    Discovers us,
        Sending a head-straight
            Tremor to the line,
Yet still presses peers
    To a splashing entry.

With the confidence
    Of talented sprinters,
        White tails bobbing,
The group emerges
    From the brush near us
And dashes across the open field,
    Past distant farm dwellings,
        To merge with
            The sloping forest backdrop. ➤

It seems a well-choreographed moment—
    Our arrival, followed by a swift
        Passing through of hooves;
Yet the randomness—and the magic—
    Of the meeting
        Is not lost to our eyes,
As we ourselves linger only briefly,
    Then vanish in our car,
        Healing the riverbank
            Of our unexpected presence,
Just as the shallow rapids
    Had healed instantly
        From the light, memorable scurry
        And asserting splash
            Of prancing hooves.

DIVINE INSIGHT

I thought I saw you in the garden
    Introducing bee to flower
Or heard your lashing, booming thunder
    Lighting skies with awesome power.

As I glimpsed the sun and mountains
    And the evening's endless glint,
I felt I knew enough without
    Deserving any further hint.

Then I saw a spotted fawn
    Walk nimbly by as birds broke day
And watched a dark cloud sprinkle rain
    And chase the butterflies away.

In the offerings around us
    I perceive an artist's touch.
Common details stir our wonder—
    Passing time reveals so much.

In the boundless beauty,
    I find miracles of love.
I sense a higher presence there
    In all of the above.

DO YOU STILL?

Passed under the desk,
    The note read,
"I love you—Do you
    Love me?"

I looked across my desk
    To yours in our group of four
        In slight embarrassment,
Not having thought
    In such a way before.

Though the note and accompanying look
    Asked for a timely response,
I could not summon or rule out
    The expected answer,
Nor authenticate its
    Attendant feeling.

Since our third grade friendship
    Leaned more to yes than no,
But clearly without the impromptu
    Certainty called for by the former,
I carefully lettered my
    Awkward left-handed reply
        With little boy terseness
And all that then mattered—
    "Yes."

Nothing happened, nothing evolved
From that moment,
Except that its safe-deposited memory,
Forty years later,
At a high school reunion,
Surfaced unexpectedly.

And, despite yours and my
Intervening lives and loves,
And with incorruptible hindsight
And honesty,
I still couldn't think of any other answer
I should have offered that day
But to say, "Yes."

DOVE OF PEACE

The peaceful music of a dove
Announces day in songs of love.
I think of moments now and past
And how these soft impressions last.

But mornings differ worlds apart,
And news events can wrack the heart.
I can't imagine facing dawn
With bombs and shrieks and loved ones gone.

Some days unfold in moments mild
Unless you are a war-torn child,
Not blessed with misted hills and peaks
But hellish scenes where horror speaks.

On wretched mornings, bleak and cold,
Mourning is an art too old,
As humans willfully engage
In devastation, blinding rage.

As dawn awakens I have heard
The dove's serene imploring word,
But all these hopeful sounds of peace
Are unfulfilled till sufferings cease.

Why can't all children everywhere
Arise to birdsongs in the air?
Why can't their fear dissolve away
So light and happiness greet day?

The dove, our nature's lofty crooner,
Rues that love can't triumph sooner.
For eons it has tolled its mission
To lift and heal our kind's condition.

EARLY SPICE

I went to the door
    To listen
And found in a faint
    Whiff of breeze
        The early spice of rain.

The slow rush of sound
    And light fragrances
        Met my senses
As sky aroused earth's
    First impression.

The damp blend
    Of leaf, grass and pollen
Steeped the moment
    With subtle aroma and recall
        And rewarded shallow inhales
            With deep return.

The confection diminished
    As rain increased,
And in a few moments
    The dilution of
        A steady drizzle
Had washed my senses
    Clear of rain's early spice.

ELEMENT OF SURPRISE

Guarding turf and territory,
    Cat of ours looks out for foe,
Watching from observer's post
    On deck until opponents show.

Certainly the end result
    Is tribute to her watchful eyes.
Her camouflaging colors
    And low crawl produce a huge surprise.

She stalks unwitting feline
    From the rail behind the hedge.
As quarry now approaches close,
    She slinks around the edge.

And when old Tom believes
    His catty influence has spread,
She takes a grand leap in the air
    And pounces on his head.

No macho mouser could fend off
    The terrorizing spell
That leaves him high falsetto
    And evicts his form pell-mell.

➤

And through the plush surroundings
    Of our woods in hot pursuit,
Two fireballs of fur
    Resolve all doubts in this dispute.

Many minutes later,
    Dainty damsel of the yard
Comes back to preen her fur
    And soon resumes her awesome guard.

ENDLESS SURF

The wind is an endless
   Breaking surf
     In the ocean of the night.

Crashing in fugue arrangements
   Along scattered wavelines,
     The rushing air
       Crescendos and wanes.

I lose myself
   In the hypnotic swells
     Of my thoughts,
Prone on the bed
   Of my dreams,
Alert in an auditory world,
   Rushing and crashing,
Strangely reassuring
   As it colors the dark
     With content
And anchors my inner seas
   With deep reflection.

EPIC OF THE SEA

I scan the fields of salt waves,
   Leveled and textured
      By morning breezes,
And squint at the shredded sun
   Bouncing up to my balcony.

Countless fins and spikes of surf
   Animate the Outer Banks seascape
And tease my inquiring vision
   With surreal sightings.

I am surprised, then, at the entrance left
   Of an endless flood of playful acrobats,
A freedom fleet of dolphins,
   Launching over, through, and under
      The warm coastal currents.

Extending their dynamic peace,
   Their buoyant harmony,
      Across the full horizon,
I absorb the spectacle,
   Their strands of nature
      Woven indelibly into my day.

Their migratory might
  Offers me an eternity
    Of splendid glances,
Broken only as pelicans,
  Cruising close to the shore,
Cross right to left
  The grain of my wonderment
    And add their own
      Low flying majesty.

Such effusion, such abundance, such grace,
  Such raw energy.

In an ocean as epic as life,
  I stand humbled and awed
    By these passings,
These divine messages
  Crossing my view
    And ennobling my day.

ESCAPE ARTIST

Robin scratching on lawn
    For early spring morsels
Darts off to high-up branch
    As you noisily unstick side door
        And head to garden.

From kitchen window,
    I view this fleet response
        To your unwitting intrusion
And admire robin's
    Quick ascent.

Would that I could
    Launch myself at will
        When startled
        Or fearing danger.

What burden to plant myself
    In front of dire news reports
        Each and every night
And not have the luxury
    To escape from my damaged peace
        In a burst of free
        And unencumbered flight.

ETERNAL SPLENDOR

Only two seats were filled
  In this car
    Of the late evening
      Commuter train.

On the opposite side of the aisle,
  Several rows back,
    Sat an attractive young lady
      Clasping her magazine,
        As I did mine.

Before long, mystery
  Filled the air,
    As sensuous scent
      Pervaded all.

My imagination amplified
  The experience,
    Romancing the aroma
      A bit more than
        The moment warranted.

The hour-long trip,
  Along with its middle-aged fantasies,
    Finally ended;
And fourteen fragrant
  Stops later,
    As we approached
      Our respective exits,
I believed that my
  Sojourn with
    The perfumed occupant
      Of the train was over.   ➤

The trip's memory
   Lingered in my consciousness
      On my drive home
         From the station
And kept stirring
   Vivid sensory impressions,
Until my wife commented
   On the pervasive odor
      Of the scent-saturated
         Eternity perfume ad
            In my People Magazine.

How can I now explain
   That nonsensical
      Digression in thought
         Back to an unusually memorable
            Evening commuter trip
               On the Long Island Railroad
Whenever anybody near to me,
   Virtually anybody,
      Wears the slightest trace
         Of that powerful potion
            Known as Eternity?

EVOKING GOD

Something smacks of God
    In the butterfly—
Its glorious stained glass
    Splashing the moment
        In ecstasy,
Surprising with raw insights,
    Composing casual miracles
        With lifts and dives,
            Glides and cartwheels.

Hardly graceful, but synonymous
    With grace and beauty,
Clustering carelessly on
    Our damp driveway mud,
Then seduced to safety
    By nectared flowers.

Nimbly navigating near objects
    And moving forms,
        Gaily courting near misses
            With walkers or drivers,
Boldly dancing in the wind,
    Spontaneous and free of concern—
Yet sadly struck by my car
    As I was heading home,
In a sudden dip of the wings,
    Glancing one carefree glider
        From front grill
            To street
And leaving in my rear view
    An abrupt break
        From a once divine day.

EXPOSURE

The moon
　　Took off
　　　　Its wrap
　　　　　　Of clouds,

Prodded by
　　Persistent puffs
　　　　Of tepid
　　　　　　Night air;

And a screech owl
　　Let loose
　　　　Its whinnied
　　　　　　Approval,

As evening
　　Turned perfect
　　　　In the revealing glow
　　　　　　Of this basking
　　　　　　　　Ball of ivory.

FABRIC

Good-bye to night;
    Tonight is gone.
A morning fire
    Fills the lawn.

A screeching owl
    Adjourns the night.
Its parting call
    Announces light.

I rush to witness
    This adieu
But catch no
    Choruses anew.

The message bearer,
    Off in flight,
Has carried off
    All trace of night

And for the gala
    Glow above
Has handed morning
    To a dove,

➤

Who from the oak's
   Inspiring seat
Proffers to dawn
   Her soft repeat.

So, with the fabric
   Still untorn,
A night is lost—
   A day is born;

And as the blue
   Is turning golder,
I so seamlessly
   Grow older.

FALL FUNERAL

Leaves bid their
Yellow, orange and red farewells
Throughout the mountains.

Across the valley,
A blue tent is visible
In the small graveyard,
Just above a line of
Newly parked cars.

Dark-suited participants
Somberly remove the contents
Of a black hearse,
Stopped in lead position.

Sun covers all surfaces,
Illuminating rites
Of nature and man.

Saturday graveside
Fills with Sunday-dressed
Participants,
Who recite scripts and responses,
Dedicating this place of rest,
Commending the spirit
To eternity.

➢

All around, vivid sunlit colors
   Respond to slight gusts
      And flutter to the ground.
Seed pods shed their cargo
   In graceful fall ritual,
      Restoring promise to the soil.

Saturday's graveside congregants
   Return to parked cars,
      Spill back down the dirt road,
        Resume their routines;
While others take down the tent,
   Refill the soil, place the headstone,
     And leave the graveyard,
      Once again,
       In quiet.

FALL NIGHT

I have a warm affection
    For the night,
A feeling for the world
    Beyond my sight.

I listen to the rhythm
    And the sound,
The light communication
    All around.

The summer noise will shortly
    Disappear.
The chilling winds are all
    That I will hear.

I'll miss the nightly chatter
    And the song,
The remnants of a season
    Far along.

I'll hear the sounds diminish
    Day by day
Until the night has nothing
    More to say.

➤

And winter will enforce
    Its stoic will
And hide the sounds of life
    Beneath its chill.

And I will long again
    For moments warm
When summer sheds all thought
    Of winter storm.

FALL OPUS

Feathered flurry of black notes
  Sprinkled from above,
Descending in gusting surges
  Onto telephone and power lines.

Waves of migratory messengers,
  Buffeted by seasonal cross-drafts,
Composing on the fly,
  Settling in patterns of random music,

Frozen in momentary high wire scores,
  Forming bleak, atonal symphonies,
Mixing frequently in wild flourishes,
  Frantic cyclones of creative force.

And then, suddenly, as if conducted
  And directed from a higher source,
Lift-off occurs, notes rip from the score,
  Ending the piece in dynamic unison.

With down-baton, the birds achieve altitude
  And spiral up and away,
To silent ovations of those in cars
  Who chanced upon this fall opus unfolding.

FAMILY PHOTO

Glossy piece of paper,
    Full of images
        Of a time,
Shedding life
    In relentless
        Radioactivity,

Decaying past its half-life,
    Slowly rushing to
        Inert emptiness,
Spent personalities
    Echoing through
        Caverns of memory
To those who form
    The current spiritual lattice
        Of long ago.

Survivors of yesterday's image
    Hold onto memory
        Until energy
            Weeps life
                From the last posing face,
And the image falls
    To others,
        Once removed,
        To preserve
            As best they can,

While they, too, occupy
    Other people-filled
        Images, just as volatile
            As the ones preceding.

FARMERS MARKET

Tented tables span
   The graveled apron,
Distilling August fields
   For view.

Judges of color and character
   Walk the booths,
Scanning baskets and boxes
   For perfect greens, yellows,
      Oranges, reds—
Plus jams, candles
   And breads.

A bit of talk
   And a proud grower's look
Qualify cucumbers
   For adoption,
Speed heads of lettuce
   To the next salad,
Send sliced squash
   To a seething boil
      On kitchen burner.

Farmers parading
   Their full colors
Convert the fruits
   Of time and skill
To earnest livelihood
   And a hopeful harvest
      Of negotiable green.

➤

The market disbands at noon,
   Tents folded up,
      Excess produce returned
      To pickup beds
         For other possible uses;
And the farmers depart
   With lighter loads
      And a sense of fulfillment
For the long hours
   Of dedicated work
      Coaxing wonders from the soil.

FAWNING FOR ATTENTION

Crowded hillside—
One full-grown turkey
Threads its brood of three
Along the forest edge,
Followed by one
Light-footed fawn
Trying to get close.

What a strange family unit
Struggling to shape itself.
How pathetic the fawn,
Testing the others
For acceptance,
Risking rebuke.

Prancing away and back
Several times,
As if it were a youthful game
To challenge protective mom,
Playful fawn trails the group
Around the hill
And out of sight,
Hoping the family elastic enough
To ignore differences
And tether one more to its train
Of trust and security.

➤

Whatever the fawn has lost
It hopes to regain
Through lithe persuasion,
As the feathery players
Consider whether
This creature of herbivore tastes
And four dancing hooves
Should join their
Scratching, pecking flock.

FELICITY

Plush tabby,
Huggy wonderful
Object of adoration,
Brandish your effusive personality
In the warm summer outdoors.
Brush passionately
Against steps leading down
To the theater entrance.

Launch your medley of colors
Over parked car rooftops,
Harmlessly padding
The shiny surfaces
To survey our progress
At intermission.

Then, dismounting, dash
To the uppermost step—
Jump up and land
Prone and writhing
For affection
On the concrete platform
Usually reserved for planters
And ornamentation.

Entice our outstretched hands
To scratch and rub
Your royal features,
As we utter endearments
And high-pitched kitty sounds.

➤

Purr in gratitude
    With half-closed eyes.
Soak in kindness
    To the limits of our attention—

Then flit off to other
    Chattering groups,
Other outstretched hands
    Ratifying your specialness,
Until the stage beckons
    All theatergoers inside
And you leave *your* showplace
    To return, exhausted, satiated,
To your own living room couch
    And the warm spotlight
        Of an obviously very loving home.

FLIGHT AT DUSK

Birds cross our sight,
  Urgent to get *there*,
    Wherever there might be.
The sun is gone,
  The sky a steel grey.
Background doves
  Keep all informed
    That night is nigh,
While birds in a rush
  Recite their lines
    One last time.

Stragglers know
  Evening is upon them
And give bats the nod
  And scoot away
    To their nests
And let the helter-skelter begin
And the blackness prevail.

FLORA AND FAUNA

Wearing only the fog of morning,
    Seeing but mist for mountains,
I stand invisibly
    In the early haze,
Culling bird sounds
    From indistinct trees and bushes.

Suited only in my natural colors,
    Posing only for empty solitude,
I inhale calmly
    From the cool,
As I watch a rabbit emerge
    From the shadows
And snowshoe closer and closer
    To my motionless form.

Deer-like, I stay in place
    And let the slight creature
        Wander by my feet
Without so much as a nod
    Of its unblinking eyes upward
        To meet mine.

In a morning in which
    I strive to blend with nature,
I am momentarily
    Inducted into it,
By a rabbit who greets me
    With no apparent interest
As if I am a stiff-legged crow
    Nonchalantly biding my time
On a hillside of wildflowers
    And tall grass.

FLYING FREE

Your golden wavy locks
    Are lifted lightly on a sea
Of gentle air in motion
    While your voice is flying free.

A nightingale of morning,
    A golden gift of song,
Your mirrored image trails a burst
    Of streaming hair so long.

The polished glass returns
    Your brush's strokes, your focused stare.
And as you tug on snares and snarls
    You're hypnotized by hair.

You blow away the moisture,
    Tame all evidence of shower.
Your voice provides the melody,
    Your flowing form the flower.

I needn't look outside today
    To contemplate the morning,
For nature's sunny presence
    Is your looking glass adorning.

FOREST TYPES

I glance at the disorder of the forest,
    Its broken and leaning hulks,
        Rotting logs and stumps,
            Upended dirt-caked roots
Sprawled among unruly sprouts,
    Optimistic juniors
        And high-reaching giants,
Easing through time,
    Plodding through seasons,
Just as animals and beings of the planet
    Mark their spaces,
        Fill their transitions,
Sprouting, thriving and ending—
    Early or late—
        As nature wills.

But the patient forest stays and waits,
    Gracefully doing time,
Watching the vibrant confusion
    Of creatures swirling about,
        Racing their clocks,
           Tallying seasons;
And this steady arboreal presence—
    As it emerges, advances, decays—
Offers a constant, reassuring force
    And witness to life.

FOREVER YOUNG

People my age
   Back then
Were ground into war
   And sprinkled over time.

People my age
   In earlier wars
Were the romantic models
   For this brutal self-sacrifice.

I was in uniform
   Back then
And rode through youth
   And its surrounding war
      Unscathed.

So spared
   In this brush
      With chance,
A strong part of me
   Now bridges all time
      With piercing empathy
For young combatants
   Caught in the
      Crush of history.

➤

No past or present war
   Allows my passive
      Involvement
Or fails to stir
   Profound hurt
That history keeps deciding
   In its ravenous way
To keep some
   Who march through its gunsights
      Forever young

And others
   Who exit its crosshairs intact
      Forever wounded.

FOUR-THIRTY-ONE

I look at my night clock,
   Its luminous digits recounting
      More than just early morning.
How many times
   Have I stirred and glanced at
      The normally plain numerals
To find a 4:31
   Smiling from the past.

So many numbers
   Have come and gone,
But only one commands
   Such primacy
That its mere presence
   Confers another point in time,
Flashes a longtime address
   With its parental presence
      In fond shorthand.

My shutter mind
   Captures that concept
      Before the "one" changes,
Allowing these two from time's past
   To begin their drift
      Through my consciousness,
Numerals no more the focus,
   Time no longer the concern,
      Love now the found feeling.

FOURTH OF JULY

Arriving darkness ignites the sky
   With fiery sparkles,
As you and I take our seats
   On the front porch steps.

Randomly erupting
   From mountains and valleys,
Colorful displays large and small
   Reward our wandering gaze.

Loudspeakers spill excitement
   From a distant rodeo
      To our spectator ears,
Celebrating with bravado and daring
   The nation's festive occasion.

Spurred by fireworks
   Throughout the evening sky,
Nearby fireflies admiringly accelerate
   Their normal evening flashes.

Then, nature's higher, more powerful,
   Pyrotechnics
Eclipse all the ceremonies and shows
   That man and insects can muster
With savage bolts
   On the horizon
And distant sky-brightening
   Events.

Even the grandest of man's displays
  Can't approach the awesome spectacle
Of the gathering storm with its
  Earth-shaking rumbles.

Passing to the northeast,
  The storm skirts our stage
And as it fades brushes us with only
  Humid, cleansing gusts.

Persistent fireflies outlast
  Man's and weather's celestial sideshows,
Carrying on with their own
  Luminous glitter
As we sift the night
  For its final golden treasures,
Reluctant to surrender
  Our front row seats.

FRONT PORCH

We sit on our front porch
    At day's end
        And watch the sun perform.
The clouds supply kindling
    As the sun ignites all,
        Splashing colors across the sky.

We savor days when the sun
    Survives weather
And we can watch its gold ball
    Dissolve into fiery patterns
        Or grow heavier until vanishing,
Smoldering its last embers
    Through the ridgeline.

Its arcing descent
    Defies talk,
Although we construct words
    To stretch our awe,
        To capture feelings,
When little else matters
    But the timeless spectacle shared.

FUNNY DANDELION

Fuzzy face upon the lawn,
    You have a most compelling need.
When a breath or breeze approaches,
    You let go of all your seed.

Once you were a yellow flower—
    Then your toupee turned to gray.
All you cared about thenceforward
    Was to send your seeds away.

You would launch them on a journey
    To another patch of earth
So as to make possible
    Another dandelion birth.

Spreading color is your purpose,
    But you have another, too.
When your seeds are launched for Patrick,
    You unleash a giggle true.

There is not a mind so fertile,
    There is not an outlook sunny
That could ever offer him
    A crazy, silly joke so funny.

➤

What it is that tickles him
    He lets all know with clarity—
Those fuzzy fliers sent asunder
    Summon pure hilarity.

When Patrick sees that pod of gray
    And Grandpa blows quite hard,
The seeds are launched up, out, beyond
    And fly across the yard.

Some jokes are good, set off a grin,
    And some have punch lines rare;
And that's the case when dandelion
    Seeds soar through the air.

GAGGLE

The geese are going out again
   Across the tops of trees.
A giddy, honking bunch above my house
   Along the breeze.

This early morning echelon,
   A frolicking formation,
Is flapping hard to keep aloft
   In miniscule migration.

I'm on the highway of their day,
   A part of each transition.
In groups of four to forty-four,
   They belly out their mission.

For me they tell of days begun
   And schedules completed.
They ride the sun and dawn awake
   And glide the rays depleted.

They launch my day with nature's touch,
   Conclude it all with wings,
Bellowing their commentary
   Over all that sings.

➤

They are a most unruly crowd,
  A daffy delegation,
Tripping over all of us
  In endless celebration.

And as they break the gentle diction
  Of the morning peace,
I hope their bright commercial
  For this life will never cease.

GHOSTS

Found in a box of correspondence
    From the 1940's and 50's,
My grandparents' letters
    To my mother—their daughter—
        Stirred up my ghosts tonight.

A two-coast family—
    With phone calls a precious
        Five dollars for three minutes
            And airfares a rare luxury—
Talked mostly through cards
    And air mail jottings
        Of daily details and feelings,
            Laden with whiffs
                Of painful separation.

I hardly recall our only
    Family trip to California,
        A long 1949 rail excursion
            When I was four.
I do remember the elegant silver train,
    The stop at the Grand Canyon,
        The cousins, aunts and uncles,
            My first brief air flight to Catalina Island,
                The old west ghost town,
And the fountain outside
    My grandparents' apartment,
        Where I watched goldfish
            With my little brother.

➤

More than my grandparents, however—
   Whom I never met one-on-one
     And whom I never visited again
      After this weeklong blitz
        Of relatives and sightseeing—
I remember the kindly old war veteran
   And his wife
     Whom I befriended
      During the lengthy return trip,
Who found my fascination
   With his lost thumb
      (Which I was convinced he was hiding)
     Quite innocent and charming.
As virtual adopted grandparents,
   They sent me a decorated
     Blue felt Mexican jacket
      After their return home,
       Which I still have
        More than sixty years later.

Through the old letters,
   Exhumed from that tattered box,
I'm sadly just starting
   To get to know
     Nana and Bampy
And sense the pathos and grief
   Of a family split between two coasts
     By a move of opportunity
      During the adventuresome 1930's.

GRAVITY

Gravity eases us out of the womb,
    Then pins us prone
      In bassinet
Where hands walk the air,
    Survey bounded space.

It is overcome
    In crawls
      And first steps
And, whoops!, plops on our behinds
    As we learn to navigate
      That rocking ship called life.

We soon walk with confidence,
    Master running,
      Accelerate into youth,
Transition into adulthood,
    Begin long journeys,
      Tread uneven time,
And, whoops!, plop on our behinds
    Occasionally
      Without warning
When our speed or pace
    Exceed our gained skills
      Or luck.

Then, ever so gradually,
    Gravity seduces us again,
      Slows us down,

➤

Reduces us
    To a virtual crawl
        And, plop!, we sometimes even fall,
As hands propel walkers,
    Wheel chairs,
Survey new bounds,
    Feel out old assumptions.

Gravity inevitably
    Leaves us prone again,
        To our dismay
            Or incomprehension,
Drawing us to the end finally
    As we drop, plop!, into soil or pyre
        And fall into inertness.

Gravity always has its way,
    No matter what we say,
As we drop into life helpless,
    Then rise, walk,
        Run, and fall,
Merely on the gravity
    Of it all.

GREAT BLUE HERON SERENADE

Under cover of dark,
  You croon your night-curdling
    Screeches
      To the forest
And shatter the sacred
  Misty silence.

You repeat your tone-deaf
  Grotesquery
    In the stage-ready stillness
      Time and again,
Tuning tastelessly for nothing
That an owl would take
  For melody.

You volume-up with confidence,
  Perfecting your delivery,
    Your ideal wakeup call
      For the dead and sleeping.

As one of those awakened,
  I listen but hear no mate
    Returning your coarse pleas,
      Assessing your raspy allure.

Perhaps your call
  Is not an entreaty
    But a plaintive report
      To the night,
        And to me,
By a solitary seabird
  In the mountains
    With nothing at all
      To sing about
        But the empty dark.

HALF MOON

Moon blares through urgent sky,
   Casting its floodlight on far mountains.
Windswept clouds charge the Big Dipper,
   Rushing over treetops.

Breezes challenge the screen,
   Rattle the window,
Inflate our room
   With exhilarating currents.

Stepping outside, I bathe in warm gusts
   And stare skyward
      Until my neck surrenders.
I celebrate time
   Hurrying by,
      Rousing my senses.

Inside, I offload night's chill
   To you,
Hear again the wind
   Strumming the screen,
      Jarring its moon-glow sheen,
See night's aura glowing on lawn
   Alongside roof's shadow,
Eye the lucent ceiling,
   And reluctantly resist
      Night's seething, frothing
         Invitation to energy.

HARDLY RAIN

It rained that day
   But in the damp
      That early May supplied
I knew despite
   The chill of droplets
      There was sun inside.

The skies were blind
   To rays above—
      The clouds effused their tears;
But all that you
   Imply to me
      The darkest moment clears.

So even as I heard
   The splashing cadence
      Of the day,
I saw the sun
   Within your heart
      And couldn't feel the gray.

HEART OF DARKNESS

Small silver bodies
  Weave frantic tapestry,
    Breaking surface,
      As hungry jaws
        Slice through them
          In the shimmering shallows.

Harbor's end bustles tensely
  In the blood rush
    Of pursued and pursuing,
      Fleeing and feeding.

We stand in their midst,
  Motionless on the trembling dock,
Apart, yet feeling almost
  A part of it,
Unchased, but not chaste
  Of excitement.

Our rush is not theirs,
  But our breath is short,
    At times withheld,
In primitive awareness
  Of the hunt,
The code of lust
  Boiling ever so closely
    Under and around
      Our civilized calm,
The seething carnage
  Occurring inches away
    In the heart of a once tame
    Darkness.

HENRY'S DOG

Henry's dog is out today—
    Crossed his street
To do a little sniffing
    Beyond his yard.

Henry's dog seldom uses
    His bark muscles now;
And when his low vision and poor hearing
    Finally do detect us,
He unleashes a mute belly paroxysm
    From his graying memory,
Unable to rock his arthritic frame
    With repeated noise bursts anymore.

His last perfunctory barks,
    Weeks back,
        Were uttered as he stood log-like,
Pointing in an illogical direction,
    Straining his ugly grimace upward
        To hear his own sound.

With Henry nursing ill-health
    Inside his house,
Henry's dog has relaxed
    His prior vigilance
Practiced so diligently
    When Henry walked the property.

➤

Now he is a silent, animated
    Child's drawing,
Appearing, then disappearing,
    From our round-the-block runs,
Just barely powering his
    Four stubby legs and drooping tail
      Across today's view.

As we cross his domain,
    Aware his paltry hulk
      Lurks there askew and unresponding,
We'd like to think he notices us today,
    Despite his fading senses,
      And then decides to let us pass
      Without a commotion.

HOLY WAR

Anthill intervening
   In a quiet picnic outing:
Thrashing feet responding,
   Never second thoughts or doubting.

Lonely evening—sitting, watching,
   Spider crossing floor.
Couldn't hurt this living thing—
   That's what compassion's for.

What circumstance can separate
   The spider from the ant?
How can I spare the spider,
   Yet his plural cousin can't?

It seems that life is sacred
   On a lonely kitchen floor;
But when I am outnumbered,
   I declare a Holy War!

HORSE SENSE

The horses are having a conference,
    A genuine nose-to-nose meeting—
A silent assemblage of faces
    Reviewing what they have been eating.

The one thing on which they're agreeing
    And seem to accept without doubt
Is that from the morning to mid-day,
    The herd still prefers eating out.

But after a morning of grazing
    On grasses worth hardly a neigh,
They return to the barn from the hillside
    To pressure the farmer for hay.

They grunt on this issue long-standing
    And snort on the problems of fall
And nod heads in 4-horse agreement
    That the field has no green shoots at all.

The farmer has run his old tractor,
    Arranging cut grass into bales,
And stirred up some real consternation
    With residents swiping their tails.

For now, eating out is not easy—
    It leaves them a little bit nervous.
The farmer must always remember—
    The fields are no longer self-service!

HOW GREAT THOU ART

Going thru the mountains,
Passing o'er the hills,
Gliding 'long the rivers,
Taking in the rills,

Tucked in certain valleys
Or propped on lofty perches,
I see a holy onslaught,
A multitude of churches.

But nothing is so notable,
So small yet looming large,
As one most humble edifice
Conducting the Lord's charge.

It has a three-space parking lot;
It sports no leaded glass;
Its pews are few in number;
Sunday crowds cannot amass.

It fills a meager footprint
In a land of many choices;
But it commands for me by far
The loudest of all voices.

For I won't find a grander name
As long as I may search
Than *New Grace Independent
Missionary Baptist Church.*

HUMMINGBIRDS

A confluence of small darting aircraft
    Visits at summer's end—
Out-of-town migrants
    Laying siege to our feeder,
        And to each other,
Belying their demure physique
    And flighty shyness.

The aeronautics
    Of split-second sallies and sorties
Suggests warfare, not welfare
    Sipped in swift drafts
        Of intoxicating sweetness.

In rough and tumble
    Near misses and collisions,
        In the air and on the feeder,
Petite teams ally their efforts
    And support each other.

Hummingbirds hover
    Before inserting needle-like bills
        Into tubes of sustaining sucrose,
Launching adversaries
    From lofty perches
        Into high-speed, unequal jousts.

Chaos ensues as winged projectiles
　　Parry their points
　　　In dynamic dogfights,
Eking only momentary rewards
　　From the feeder's precious reserve.

The day is a far cry
　　From the serene summer visits
Of resident Ruby Throats
　　Enjoying treats of the season,
Whose fleet forms have just left
　　To join the migration
And who are now part
　　Of this urgent flight
　　　From impending winter.

Migrating from this, their land of plenty,
　　They, too, must compete on the way
　　　For an increasingly scarce
　　　　Migrant's fare,
Just as these passers through
　　Vie for end-of-season's
　　　Rare nectar.

HURRY, DOGWOOD

Hurry, dogwood,
    Forest soon
Spills earth tone buds
    And newborn greens.

Decorate your limbs
    In white,
And dress up nature's
    Early scenes.

Find your sun,
    Reflect your light
On forest edge,
    In woodland deep.

Stretch out through
    The tardy bloomers—
Make your mark
    While others sleep.

Time is rushing.
    Spring is ready.
Soon your neighbors
    Will arrive.

Spread your gifts
    In lacy patches,
Telling all
    That you're alive.

I ALSO RAN

My steps across
    The decades span.
The children dash—
    I also ran.

Across the lawn
    They improvise.
They spin and weave
    Like butterflies.

Their dreams and actions
    Neatly blend.
Their energies
    Drive their pretend.

In my heart
    I want to be
A thought creation
    Flying free.

I'd settle for
    No other plan,
For in my youth
    I also ran

And saw how truly
    All things flow
On fleeting wings
    Of never know

➤

And how an impulse
    Anchors down
When spirit wears
    Adulthood's frown

And turns to dreaming
    Wistfully
Of lawns so green
    And legs so free.

ICE FLOES

The harbor wears
    A necklace of ice,
Its rocky facets
    Heaved up by the tides.

As salt water fills
    The depleted slopes
        Of shoreline,
Ice creaks up
    And nature overwrites
        Its last work.

Fields of snow
    Stretch across
        Unresponsive water,
And ducks and gulls
    Trudge the frosted surface
        To watery windows of thaw
        Etched by springs.

Winter blows its icy breath
    And stills the harbor's
        Ripples and waves
            With temporary death,
Coating nature
    In desolate beauty.

➤

A cormorant catches my eye,
   Disappearing repeatedly
      Under the surface
         Into the harbor underworld
Through a ringlet of water
   At dock's end.

The encumbrance of winter
   Will extend
      For the balance of January,
         And beyond February;
But hope will carry us longer,
   Until spring dissolves
      Persistent jewels of ice,

Giving the tides back
   Their effortless motion
And the birds back
   Their carefree plunges
      From the blue.

IDEAS

Ideas sit on my shoulders,
   Nuzzling me for attention,
     Whispering phrases,
      Flashing images.

Then they sit on my head,
   Scratching gray-splashed crown
     With barnyard claws,
      Unwilling to surrender.

Then they rip
   Other priorities out
     At the roots,
      Steal any focus
       But their own;

And, finally, they hijack time,
   Enslave thoughts,
     Indenture purpose,
      Confine being
        To the oft-times impractical,
        But urgent, notion
That they will add
   Flesh and substance,
     Girth and breadth,
      Even some permanence,
To the diaphanous,
   Anchorless ether
     Of human consciousness.

I'M ONLY A CLOUD

I bury my gaze
   In the blue of the sky.
I'm just a mere puff
   Floating over and by.

I am a lone sentinel
   Spiriting through.
I'm now cast away
   On an ocean of blue.

I'm only a cloud
   In the loftiest place.
I'm drifting away
   From the wind's gusty face.

By dusk all my vapor
   May fade and be gone.
I may not be there
   For the glory of dawn.

I'm only a vision,
   A vestige of tear,
Pursuing a dream
   Until I disappear.

IMAGINARY MORNING

Early fog
    Loads up leaves
      With imaginary rain,
Spilling, tipping, cascading
    Their contents windlessly
      Into thirsty earth.

We walk our mountain lane,
    Repeating our hill climb—
Up and down,
    Up and down—
As morning comes alive
    In the mist.

Our exercise stirs repeated whistles
    From high-up bobwhite,
      Hailing elusive cab,
And cues our trusting rabbit
    To breakfast at his usual spot
      Near our footsteps.

With a bulbous outward eye,
    This tawny bystander records
      Our ascents and descents
        Sidling across his delectable patch,
Sensing our indifference—
    Tuned to our sounds.

➤

The settling fog
   Dampens our hair,
      Wets the savory grass,
Kisses everything—
   Hugging valley and ridgeline.

Deer on forest fringe
   Snort their disapproval of us,
      Fleeing down adjacent trail.
Pileated woodpecker
   Shrieks its arrival,
      Then knocks around treetops
         And bug-filled crevasses.
Squirrels sprint across branches,
   Shaking nuts from trees,
      Scooting down to forest floor
      To bury their bounty.

Fall sweatshirts come off
   As we pump ourselves warmer
      In the chill morning air,
Expressing our nature,
   In nature,
      Repeatedly,
         For forest locals to see.

IMAGININGS AT A LAUNDROMAT

Half the machines
    Whir and tumble
This Sunday evening
    At the laundromat.

Three immigrant families
    Populating the floor
Advance robust loads of laundry
    From bags to washers
To dryers to bags again
    Over the next hour and a half.

Their well-behaved,
    Brightly togged children
        At knee level
Carom from parent to parent
    Soaking up kind words and smiles,
        Along with mock sternness.

My own lights and darks
    Glance over washer spindles
Into hyper-clean tanks
    In separate loads.

➢

While water and detergent
   Attack the imaginings of dirt
      On my hardly soiled clothing,
I open up my free culture/arts newspaper
   On the humid porcelain lid
      Above the swirling darks.

By this time, a profane local couple
   And their profane
      Waist-high son
Sprawl at the other end
   Of the facility on the room's
      Only benches and table.

The lean, fast-talking,
   Endlessly smoking wife rattles on
To her sullen, massively boyish husband
   In words their almost-as-profane
      Son is apparently used to.

As I scan the paper's schedules and ads,
   Describing New Age, mystical,
      And diverse cultural happenings
With their longing for spiritual health
   And revitalization,

I attend this rare, impromptu
    Cultural event
Amidst an orchestra
    Of whirring machines
And a dash of local
    And foreign dialects.

I lock myself into a rinse cycle
    Of reader invisibility
As I lean on my machine,
    Self-consciously suspended between
Extreme promises of spiritual awakening
    And the unavoidable perception
        Of a wider world
With beliefs and assumptions
    Unsuited for the alternate universes
        Displayed with such confidence
            In my culture/arts newspaper.

IN THE SHOWER

In the shower
    Standing there,
Head is bowed
    As if in prayer.

Soothing sound
    Of chanting rain,
Disappearing
    Down the drain.

Meditation,
    Inundation,
Stimulating
    Circulation.

In between
    The world and dreaming,
Free association
    Streaming.

Mystery of
    Steam ascending,
Bliss like this
    Should be unending.

Rich in thoughts,
    Reflecting there—
True harmony
    Pervades the air.

INDUSTRY

Slitting, patterning, assembling,
    Needles sewing, motors whirring—
Echoes of what came before,
    Visions of the past recurring.

There's another occupation;
    There's another workforce lurking.
Off in corners, tucked in rafters,
    Spider craftsmen still are working.

Thirty years of new apparel
    Fell down chutes to bins below.
Ironed smooth, then bagged and boxed,
    They went to stores in constant flow.

Now the deft machines are silent,
    Workers' hands don't push and pull.
Garments no more tumble finished;
    Canvas bins no more are full.

There's a sequel now beginning—
    Humans have new tasks begun.
Sewing silenced yields to printing,
    New impressions to be run.

Life is locked in constant labor.
    Generations come and go.
Industry may grow and falter;
    Yet spiders bustle, high and low. ➤

In the corners, cracks and rafters,
    Layoffs didn't stop that crew.
Only death concludes their season.
    Only birth can hire anew.

They would cover all in webbing,
    Clothe geometry in fuzz,
Capture every moth and mite
    And quell each flight and angry buzz,

But for human toil competing,
    Foiling artisans of edges,
Whisking off their woven fibers,
    Ridding filaments from ledges.

When they coexist with humans,
    Sheer persistence stalls the fight.
Neither wins and neither loses.
    Neither frees its foe from sight.

Stalemate is the rule of order;
    Sharing is the rule in force;
Industry is what you call it
    When persistence stays its course.

INTO THE NIGHT

I bid good night to night
From upstairs balcony
And pause to listen
To the almost silence.

Everyone sleeps
And the moment is my own.
I stand motionless
In the outdoor chill,
Time of no essence.

I feel as if I am waiting
For something—
I feel the night has
One more thing to say.

Then, down the snow-covered lawn at left,
Beyond the row of bushes,
Scurries a fox
On his familiar ground.

He cuts the corner
As he turns left
And patters down the tidal beach
Toward occasional distant sounds
Of nesting ducks and geese.

I sense the impending drama
As I imagine his instinct's draw
To the feathery flock down shore,
Hunger driving him
Toward the ultimate prize.

➤

Minutes later, baritone geese from afar
    Trumpet their alert,
Apprising all
    Of the slinking shadow
        Dangerously approaching.

Opportunity thus lost,
    No fowl dinner this night
Caps off urgent hunt
    Of prowling predator.

Memory of last week's
    Curdling screech
        In the night
Reminds me that failure
    Is not always
        The final act
Of this fox's forays
    Into the black.

How long till vigilance fails
    Geese and ducks
And rewards coldly patient,
    Cooly persistent visitor
        On his nightly rounds?

Only the darkness knows
    This grim secret.
Only error, or illness, or age
    Will designate who shall next fill
        The fox's night with bounty.

JANUARY SUN

A robust wind shakes trees,
　As sun streams across morning's table,
　　Contradicting outside roar.

House's windowed enclosure
　Draws in solar warmth,
　　While straining and creaking
　　　At each gust.

Welcome rays that defy winter outside,
　Produce unwelcome candor inside;
As hands on table,
　Basking in brilliance,
　　Divulge lines, hairs, wrinkles, spots
　　　And a palette of flesh tones.

Then, just as angled sun
　Would exaggerate shifting desert sands,
It exposes face's
　Surface features and tints
　　To light's critical gaze,
Revealing a salting of grays
　Over sags, wrinkles,
　　And protests of age.

➤

This new day's sun,
  As it celebrates warmth
  And the passage of night—
  Rebuking wind,
        Abetting indoor calm—
Subtly shifts the mood
  With its vivid spotlight on
  The undeniable truths of age.

JESSIE

Dog presence,
Sprawled out
Around entryway
At day's end,
Obstacle to patrons
Picking up cars,
Oblivious to all
But that one
Significant person.

Light sleeping monitor
Of casual comments,
Stretching off
Kind words,
Cordial pats,
Careful steps around
Outstretched ears,

Only tuned for
That smell,
That sound,
That touch,
At the end
Of the workday
That says,
"It's time to go home,
Jessie."

JUDITH

Outside—
    A friend of flowers—
You coax beauty
    From the earth.

Inside,
    Your light hands
Coax song
    From keys
And from the youthful voice
    At your side.

Your spirited,
    Nature-fed music
Lifts all around
    From care.
Your bright mood
    Dances us through
        And stills urgent time—
Your blush of smile
    Our rush of joy.

Our hearts focus
    On the moment—
Spread so wide it intersects
    All of memory;
And in this poignant present—
    This flight of
        Voice and fancy—
The melody of the moment
    Plays on
        Without end.

JUST ONCE

I gazed upon my life
   And sensed its rush before my time.
I saw my youth dissolving
   Long before I met my prime.

I felt the moment slipping by,
   My stay on earth depleting.
I saw the present hurrying,
   My mortal cares repeating.

I feared that I would squander time
   And miss my only chance.
I didn't want to waste
   The opportunity life grants.

We occupy this planet
   For a brief allotted hour,
And there exists within each heart
   A reservoir of power.

My hope is to define it well,
   Try not to let it slide.
My challenge is to pull some meaning
   From this force inside.

Sitting near the edge of time,
   My mind forever hunts
To justify the simple truth—
   We pass this way just once.

KING OF LITTLE FISH

Standing on railing,
  Sighting straight down
    Along pointed beak,
Belted Kingfisher
  Studies rippled surface
    Ten feet below.

This brush businessman,
  Crew-cut king of little fish,
    Is all concentration
As he guards this patch of thaw,
  Awaiting the moment
    When minnows return.

Silver school
  Flashes into his gaze
    And, laser-like,
He cuts through the air
  To incise one minnow's space
    And seize it from being.

He returns to his clutch of rail
  With shiner pinned immobile—
Then gulps it down live
  In one deft toss.

He arranges himself
  With a shake and a shrug
And extends his crest
  Brush-high
    To semi-dry
      In the frosty air.

Then, back to business,
　　As he huddles his gaze downward
　　And transfixes on the moment,
Decoding ripple from wave,
　　Light breeze from
　　　Swirling light fin.

Again and again
　　His hors d'oeuvres
　　Are served by the current,
And he dives athletically
　　For them,
　　　Only sometimes missing.

As bite-sized nibbles
　　Accumulate into
　　A gorging meal,
Satiated Kingfisher
　　Halts his ritual,
　　　Launches onto a piling,
　　　And briefly preens.

Departing more quietly
　　Than on his shrieking,
　　　Hunger-edged arrival,
He swoops off
　　To his high-up lair
And settles into
　　A hard-earned
　　　Afternoon peace.

LADIES OF LIGHT

Ladybug litter
    In lights and on ledges—
Dry speckled cases,
    Now hollow and still—

Hard to distinguish
    From those vital players
Who worship the sunbeams
    On bright window sill.

The relics remaining
    With spirit now missing
Foreshadow the subsequent
    Pill dots of lust.

These eager arrivals
    Are lives in a hurry,
Running their cycle
    So deftly toward dust.

And the bright orange shells,
    Once driven by purpose—
Seeking white surfaces,
    Lured by the sun—

Now huddle together,
    Stripped of their passions—
Brittle, yet much like the living
    When done.

LAUNDRY DAY

Banners of wet laundry stretch their colors
From two levels
Of small, time-worn apartments,
The pastels, denims and patterns,
In a family of sizes,
Spritzed redundantly by rain.

Toy-strewn walkways and yard
Are idle until school lets out.
A tardy sun will crisp and brighten
Damp garments
For use again
In the energies of living.

The sprawling time capsule
Of a yard
Is more than playground,
With its scattering of
Discarded appliances,
Rain beading on the rusty porcelain.

A car hulk is permanently planted
Beyond the designated asphalt—
Now empty of parked vehicles—
Its flat tires nesting
In the coarse yellow grass.

No pride of ownership stirs the soils
With patchwork gardens,
Repairs worn carpentry,
Renews flaking paint.   ➤

Without the blowing fresh laundry,
    It would seem a ghost town,
Awaiting further decay
    And destruction.

The expected hubbub of afternoon
    Will arrive and dissolve
        Before I retrace my highway route
        In later hours.
The kids at play will be reeled in
    Along with the fresh-smelling laundry,
As the parking lot will again fill
    With pickups,
        Back from the day's work.

I wonder if the upcoming highway expansion,
    With its planned assault
        On the dwelling's frontage,
Will dash and doze the relics
    Of building and place,
Leaving only this vivid memory
    Of laundry day banners
        Stretching in celebration
Of the routine
    Comings and goings
        Of a handful of
            Working class families.

LEAVES

How they fall
    In fall—
Leaden large,
    Light and lithe,
        Zig and zag, up and down,
            Sporty spiral,
                Pirouette-in-place,
                    Slicing diagonal,
Crimson,
    Orange
    And yellow.

All in all
    An autumn ball
    Free for all.

Nothing stalls
    The levity,
        The pull of earthly gravity.

Such gratitude for season's kiss—
    The fall should always
    Be like this.
I can't dismiss this sight at all—
    Amazing how they fall
    In fall.

LETTING GO

On this still September day,
    With yellow and orange leaves
      The exception,
A turning leaf lets go
    And plummets straight down
      Without a flutter.

This streak of bright
    Against the green,
      Ahead of season,
        With no breeze to trip it,
          Puzzles with its leaden plunge.

The seasons compete and overlap,
    But this early leaf
      With no reason of wind
        And only the gravity of color
Is the mysterious tuning note
    For an extravagant time and season
      Soon to be.

LIGHTS ACROSS THE VALLEY

You have stolen the night,
  Not this night,
For the moon forces through
  Tonight's swift river of clouds
    With its competing lamplight.

But you dot the valley
  Needlessly
    With powerful beacons
Garishly undoing
  The mute, black emptiness
    With its glittering cargo.

Tonight moans eerily
  And creaks the house,
    As fields and mountains
      Bathe in moonlight;
And stars await another night
  To display their mysteries.

But lights across the valley
  Sound out shamelessly
    As paid sentinels
      Of security
And distract on nights
  When the moon rests
    And the majesty of eternity
      Sparkles overhead.   ➤

How sad to dissolve the night
  And divert attention
    To earthly beacons
When endless diamonds
  Spill across the universe
    And beckon us to focus elsewhere.

LISTEN TO THE QUIET

Listen to the quiet,
　　To an evening drained of sound,
To the silence of the heavens,
　　To the moon glow all around.

Hear the trees in silhouette
　　As shadows cast their gray,
As leaves extend their greenery,
　　As insects wait for day.

Tune in to the fragrant smells,
　　The still of birds in slumber.
Watch a cloud move into place,
　　A waning star encumber.

Place yourself out in the night
　　When sound has gone away,
And listen to the quiet
　　As it gathers strength for day.

LITTLE GIRL

Little girl with golden curl
   And words of pure invention,
Share with me your precious world—
   Immerse me with attention.

Bother me with wonder;
   Encumber me with awe;
Tickle me with nonsense
   In everything you draw.

Distract me with your interest
   In everything I do.
Pour out your emotions
   When your little heart is blue.

Tease me with your fantasies;
   Let bright impressions shine.
Bathe me with your knowledge;
   And deliver me from mine.

Carry me as passenger
   In a wagon made for two.
Remind me we will always be
   Just children passing through.

LITTLE ONE

Talking to "Gram"
 As front lawn's
  Tender autumn sun
   Lulls itself
    Through leafy gold,
Little one lights
 The still air
  With her calm,
   Precise tones.

"Gram" bends her gaze
 And her speech
  Downward
To engage her
 Fresh-eyed equal.

Our morning walk
 Hurries past
  Their tranquil
   Openness,
Not locking
 Into content,
  Nor moving
   Another glance
    Into their mood,

➤

But grateful
    That the fullness
        Of fall's message
Included a
    Passing reminder
        Of "Gram"
            And her little one,
Majestic gold
    With vibrant green,
        Coexisting so brilliantly.

LITTLE WREN

Little wren,
Your nest preparing,
Agitated thoughts
Declaring,

With melodic
Commentary,
Spend your grand
Vocabulary.

Chiding, dusting,
Singing, cleaning—
Bowl of thickets
Loudly preening.

Virtuoso
Talents raining,
Spilling over,
Rich complaining.

With your energy
Effusive,
Darting music
So elusive,

➤

I can hardly
    Fix a glance
On your lively
    Little dance.

But I'll catch,
    With hidden glee,
Your tiny little
    Symphony.

LOSS OF THE SUN

I will miss the sun.
    It has bathed this winter day
        With an unexpected 60 degrees.
It has defied the rainy forecast
    And filled all eligible rooms
        With sunbeams
           In proper sequence.

It hurries to the horizon,
    Blinding to our eyes,
Graciously letting ferns
    In our west-facing bathroom
        Bask in a final splash of rays.

So complete is our bond
    With the winter sun
        That we rue day's end,
           The fast approaching dark,
Especially those hollow moments
    Just after sun's passing,
        Its descent to another day
           To others who gain from our loss.

The luminous ferns
    Mourn in luscious afterglow;
        And I wish I could have extracted
        Their full euphoria
           From the sun's presence,
As I feel their letdown
    At its demise.

LOST ACRE

Bulldozer backs down flatbed ramp,
    Turns to face dense, green acre,
And launches hungry blade
    In crunching, snapping passes
Of ruthless, unstoppable
    Energy.

Trees loudly protest their
    Ripping roots, breaking sinews,
        Toppled histories.

Nests plummet, their steadfast supports
    Pushed, ground and chain sawed
        Into massive pyres of kindling.

Snakes and turtles,
    Rodents and insects
        Succumb to indiscriminate carnage;
Death and rebirth end
    In one final scouring.

Earth bleeds black humus
    From the settled leaf cover
        Of falls past.

Choice lumber is lifted onto trucks,
    Lugged to sawmills,
Debarked and ripped
    To perfection.

Leftover traces of forest
Ascend in the smoke
Of a dry day
And a can of gasoline.

The last evidence of
This thriving patch of life
Is entombed in ruddy soil,
The charred remains
Dozed invisible
In one mass grave.

A few token oaks,
Naked survivors of human scourge,
Stand as embarrassed,
Out-of-the-way reminders
Of a past life—

A considerable history
Blown away in smoke,
Ground into wood chips and dust,
Pared into studs and beams.

One lovely acre: stripped and ready
For the hammers and nails,
The pourings and plantings,
The habitat to end all habitats.

LOST CALF

A gut-driven cry
    Interrogates the valley
As to the whereabouts
    Of her lost calf.

Repeated again and again,
    The only acceptable answer
Is the valley's offer
    Of a welcoming bellow in reply.

The hills hold their breath
    And flowing waters listen,
Yet only silence greets
    The maternal longings.

No imploring will pull them
    Back together;
And a mother's rightful demands
    Change into anguish,
        Telegraphed to all of nature.

LOST CAT

Faded message,
  Tacked to trees
    And telephone poles
Flashes loss
  And hopeful waiting,
    Aged painfully into grief.

Weathered reminders
  Of "Sunshine,"
    The black calico
      With orange and white speckles,
Bid us imagine between terse lines
  And conjure the purr, the play,
    The pressure on the feet
      At bed's end,
The private moments
  Bonding pet to person,
The light talk
  In language
    Fondly phrased,
The caring, the comfort,
  The companionship,
    The warmth exchanged.

➤

All this, set between simple lines,
   In poignant posting
      For all to see,
         For all to mourn
            In modest measure,
Catching rays
   That "Sunshine" cast
     So touchingly
        As to greet us
           In tributes along the way.

LOVE BEYOND WORDS

I've gotten beyond words.
    Touch is my translator,
      My new native tongue,
Used and reused through the years
    To give carbon its dignity,
      Time its searing now,
        Us our universe.

I surrender words
    When I surrender to you
      And you refresh
        Our common language,
Learning it again, as before,
    Surrendering to me,
      To my touch,
        As if it were new.

Words are the threshold of night,
    Or morning,
      Or awakening at any hour,
Or sometimes they don't exist at all,
    And touch is all,
      And the spoken is insufficient
        To express the inexpressible;
And we both understand our new tongue
    And let words rest
      And let touch explore once more
        The inexpressible.

LOYAL BUMBLEBEE

Fading bursts of yellow
   Still attract the bumblebee,
The rhododendron blossoms
   Stirring flights of reverie.

What once deserved minute inspection
   Of each clustered flower
Now is but a rain-diminished
   Glimpse of former hour.

Early blooms are edged in brown;
   A scant few hold their color.
The intervening days of rain
   Have turned majestic duller.

The wilted blooms seduce no more
   This bumblebee attending
Whose flight is more selective now
   As plentied feasts are ending.

What touches is the bumblebee's
   Unerring dedication
To this object of pure love
   Now facing transformation.

The intimate relationship
   That draws the bee inside
Keeps up until the final bloom
   On its last branch has died.

It's hard to measure minute feelings
   As a mere observer,
But one can sense the start and end
   Of this small player's fervor.

And nearby understanding hearts
   Can carry the belief
That as the final flower fades
   This bee feels loss and grief.

MÄDCHEN

Hearing my characteristic sound-presence,
   Mädchen lumbers over
     From neighbor's yard
To seek her soul-mate,
   Her ball-throwing extra,
     Her synonym for silly play—
       Me.
Still carrying her winter coat,
   Less than lithe
     With her touch of flab,
She summons her essential puppiness
   And flatters me with
     One saliva-slick ball
      Held vice-like in offering.
That she has picked me
   With her abundance of family
     And her always-loving home environs
Touches my day
   And jogs my nostalgia
     For the shadowy canine presence
      Of my own past.
That she picks me to tease this day
   With her slathered-on sphere,
     By eager tugs, perpetual keep-aways,
     And occasional fetches,
Places me in her youthful past,
   And her in mine,
     As I place my hands trustingly
      In her incisored grip.

Our fearless sparring
    Connects our childhoods,
        Free-spirited and universal.
Puppy to puppy,
    Our past replays its memories
        Through fingers in jaws,
            Through tease and counter-tease.
And then, as age calls us back to our day,
    She reluctantly brings her ball home,
        Retaining this ticket of spirit,
            This reminder and reason
For traversing yards,
    Crossing borders,
        And drawing the past out of me again
            In tugs and pulls
                And friendly skirmishes
                    Some day soon.

MAKE MY DAY

Scruffy little bird
   Quite near the curb—
     Demeanor rude—
Facing passersby with one
   Pure puff of attitude.

Waiting for her restaurant
   To open up its doors
And send to outdoor tables
   Breakfast platters she adores.

Table tidbits of
   The morning clientele
     Will fall.
A ripped off piece of toast
   Will often answer her
     Shrill call.

It takes an educated bird
   To work the pavement smartly—
A prof of outside eating traits
   To egg on patrons heartily.

And waitresses will also help
   As they wipe off the tables.
Each tipping client up above
   A "tip" below enables.

Rewards of all this table fare
  Are quite a haul for one,
But when the late arrivals fly in,
  Plenitude is done.

Handouts are abundant
  When this tiny miss first comes;
But she knows best the truth—
  The early bird receives the crumbs.

MAY I?

May I,
    Said April to spring,
Unwrap your gifts
    And open everything?

If you proceed ahead,
    Maintain your way
And stay determined—
    Yes, of course, you may.

But if you don't advance
    And shed the past,
You cannot open up
    This treasure vast;

And though the sun assumes
    A higher arch,
You'll have to yield to May
    If lost in March.

MELLOW DAY

Damp, dull,
    Lazy day.
Only crow has
    Words to say.

Halting rain
    Discards its dew.
Singing birds
    Have slipped from view.

Sun is napping
    In the clouds.
Trees are dressed
    In mottled shrouds.

Far too warm
    This mellow day
To warn of summer
    Cast away.

Fall is waiting
    In the wings.
Prudent is
    The heart that sings,

Taking in
    This tepid prize
Before the drift
    Of summer flies.

MELODY OF MORNING

What is it about the
　　First hint of morning
　　　　In the damp, dark fog
　　　　　　Of late April,
In the warm chill
　　That could have been colder
　　　　Here in the mountains,

That launches the tiny woodwinds
　　In our trees,
　　　　Tuning, celebrating
　　　　　　Their high-pitched instruments.

Then the dove, cello-like,
　　Bows its calm wisdom
　　　　Over the excited chatter,
And the percussive
　　Antique auto-horn
　　　　Of the rooster
　　　　　　Rouses the flock repeatedly
　　　　　　　　As if to make a point,

And the tone-deaf
　　One-note caw of the crow
　　　　Calls his kind,
　　　　　　Heralding himself
　　　　　　　　Over the music
　　　　　　　　　　Atop the highest tree,
Swooping in animated flight
　　To another high branch.

What baton of imperceptible
    Luminescence
      Shines in the east
        Through blinding fog
To give morning its downbeat,
    The hiding orchestra
      Its optimism.

What composer hands
    This concert to me
      As I crack the door
        To listen
          In the fading dark
           Of morning.

MEMORY'S PLACES

In memory's far ranging
    Unpredictable revealing,
I encounter surface features,
    My topography of feeling.

I see the total substance
    Of a period of time
Reflected in the simple space
    Through which impressions climb—

A geologic slice of life,
    A spirit-filled cross section,
A tactile meeting with the past,
    An image for detection.

For years, I darted down and up
    A root-filled path of dreams.
My youth enjoyed the sanctuary
    Of this path, it seems.

And now as I confront
    The tender features of my past,
I'm pleased that places such as this
    In hallowed thoughts still last.

MEMORY'S TODAY

Some time in the mist
    Where tomorrow stays
I'll visit in spirit
    My yesterdays.

Off in the future
    Where special things last,
I'll relish in quiet
    This touch of the past.

I'll journey through time,
    Draw the chaff from the wheat,
And light upon moments
    I'd like to repeat.

And while I am drifting
    Through memory's way,
I'll pause and I'll savor
    My thoughts of today.

MESSENGER

Your soil freshly packed,
　　Your stone newly set,
Your feline spirit watches over us
　　From your favored hillside perch.

The expectation of you
　　Is still with us,
Your brush of fur
　　Still resident at our feet.

We wake to an empty house,
　　Still feeling the details of your care,
Still tempering our life
　　With consideration of you.

We feel naked with your
　　Sudden departure
　　　　To nearby hillside—
The lost pathos of your stare,
　　Your soft meow gone,
　　　　Your scant weight
　　　　　　Unfelt in our laps.

Your first morning
　　Free of physical bonds
Brings us your risen spirit
　　In the mystical form
　　　　Of a never-before-seen
　　　　　　Hummingbird,
Hovering in branches
　　Above your stone.

We feel odd
    As we propose your soul's
        Transmigration
From minimal cat
    To diminutive bird.

Comfort flows strangely
    From this symbolic presence;
And we take the little messenger
    As a heartening lift-off
        Of a life lost—
A light boost
    To left-behind hearts
        Struggling to fill the emptiness.

MILKY WAY

A softly trailing veil
   Lays its delicate fabric
     Across the sky,
Riding currents gracefully
   Across night's remarkable clutter.

The cold, sparkling vastness
   Contrasts with my inner warmth
Bathing naturally
   In the tepid summer air.

Returning to my covers, I feel the reality
   And supplementing warmth
     Of forms pressed together
And carry with me that moment—
   Under cover of night—
     When I gazed into
       A limitless reality.

At times like this
   It is not enough for me
     Just to retire at night
To the warm security
   Of covers and touch
Without first acknowledging
   The complex mystery
     Of 'out there.'

This genuflect—
    This spiritual nod to the heavens,
      Prayer without words—
Strangely comforts
    My earth-taut mind,
Lets me channel outward,
    After funneling inward
During a day's noise
    And distraction.

It pulls me from the temporal earthly
    To the universal other—
And then returns my chilly outer skin,
    Brimming yet with warmth,
      Bathed in awe,
To the renewed miracle
    Of my own inner space.

MIRROR

Flash pan of spent images,
    What memories do you hold
        In your silvered silence?
What soul-searching glances
    Have bounced back;
What pathos have you whispered
    To your twin;
What tears un-shed
    Have you insightfully read;
What brash confidences
    Have you shared
Or theatrically hammed out
    That no one sees?

What flesh have you scrutinized,
    Evaluated, berated, praised,
        Before it slips into
            The steaming shower;
What candid scenes
    Has your looking glass
        Cherished and framed,
            Fixed and frozen
                In your Edenic album?

What together moments,
    Lusty poses, racy excesses,
        Passionate interludes
Have you logged
    With explicit honesty?

What stories have entered
   Your labyrinth,
Mirroring beauty, caring,
   Candor, strife,
     Details of days, lives, pasts,
Only to be swallowed instantly
   In visual amnesia.

Witness and voyeur,
   Confidante and critic,
     Window into the soul,
       Chronicler of the heart,
You could easily shatter
   For the burden you carry,
Or cloud up with intimate moments
   You have witnessed,
Were you truly reflective
   And not freed from concern
     By the icy ease of
       Your forgetting.

MISTY MOOD

Rain taps the deck,
   Bursting its wet breath
      Through slider screen.

Wife beats out fitness
   To the rhythm of
      Lithe TV leader.

Cat conserves energy,
   Standing gaze-less
      And tummy-full
         On marble haunches
            An arm stretch away.

I imbibe my leather chair
   And pull these elements
      Of luscious peace
         Together
            Into a mood.

MOCKINGBIRD

Mockingbird—
    Little master of
        Many tongues—
Meeting us
    Morning after
        Morning
With brazen song
    From the same
        Stooping branch,

You are a sentinel,
    A soloist,
        A performer,
Plucking our attention
    From our early pace,
Lifting our eyes
    From the hypnotic
        Pavement.

You lift and turn
    And flutter
        Your slate colors
        At us
As we slow
    In salute;

And as we stride
    Beyond,
We carry your music
    In our thoughts
And your generosity
    Into our day.

MOM

That night I asked the stars
    If you were there—
        And they replied,
And then I asked again—
    And you replied;

And many times since
    I have asked,
        If only to say hello,
And get no reply—
    As tonight,
When no meteor lit
    My slice of sky
        Between trees and house.

But what I don't know,
    Yet suspect,
Is that somewhere,
    Beyond the limits of my sight,
A friendly streak of light
    Is signing on to my thoughts,
Signaling an answer
    To my undying question,
Unable to expand our brief
    Moment of synchronicity
        In this life—

Until, that is, my own flash of light
    Replies back,
        Streaking its earthly finale;
            And our skies become one.

MONUMENT TO TIME

When my father, in his nineties,
  Moved to a nearby senior residence,
    His cat came to live with us;
And the two got to see
  Each other often.

Eight years after Dad's passing,
  His tabby moved with us
    To another state
And, as an older pet
  In a new location,
Was cautious about
  Where she went.

She seldom ventured beyond
  The flat, sun-drenched rock
    On the hill behind our house,
Where she soaked in warmth
  To comfort her tired frame
And kept an eye on us
  Down below,
    Framed in the large
      Kitchen windows.

She, too, eventually left us,
  And we placed her
    Under the rock
Where she had spent
  So much of her time.   ➤

In this serene spot
    She was now time's sentinel,
      Watching over us still
As the years slipped by
    And memories moved
      Further away.

Surprising was our recent discovery
    That the once small hemlock
      On the edge of her hilltop clearing
Had spread its boughs
    Beyond her flat rock,
      Almost blocking the sun
        And erasing the stone from view—
Reminding us how time could ease
    So painlessly by
And unassumingly overreach
    Its humble monuments
      Of spirit and space.

MOONGLOW

The moon is almost full.
  The sky is almost clear.
The night is hardly old.
  The cold is hardly there.

I'm tuned into the night.
  I'm standing in the air.
I'm only dressed for sleep.
  My legs and arms are bare.

I hear the hooting owl
  Relaxing in his call.
The valley is his instrument
  In hollow nights of fall.

The melody is haunting,
  The repetition spare.
The night has one performer
  In shadows of moon glare.

I seem the only audience
  Across from distant stage.
My keen appreciation
  Sends an insufficient wage.

But I will pay in memory—
  Imagination's flight—
For what I stand and listen to
  And cannot see tonight.

MOONSET

Mimicking death,
    The full moon meshes
        With a tree-line
Stripped by mid-fall
    Of its lush growth.

Ever so slowly,
    In the cold, dark morning,
        The golden orb
            Dissolves away,
Emulsified by bare branches
    And trunks
Until the heat of its bold descent
    Lingers only in faint afterglow.

I watch the sinking moon's
    Phosphor fade away,
As decades earlier
    My mother's waning pulse
        Stretched forever
            To meet her final horizon
                And shed her precious last heat.

How many times
    Will that moment
        Set in my soul
            In unexpected metaphors
And slice the golden orbs of memory
    Into radiant last strands
        And soft afterglow?

I let an impending sunrise
   Lift my thoughts
      As the eastern sky lightens
        For sun's entry,
         Day's rebirth,
And I trade the parting warmth
   Of final glow
      And last breath
        For the optimism of day
          And the wholeness of memory.

MORNING MAGIC

Tents surprise us on the grassy,
　　Winter-bleached hillside,
　　　　Catching morning's first rays.

Like floating magic carpets or
　　Little gray clouds,
They are piloted by artisan spiders,
　　Nightlong weavers of gossamer,
Who build beauty and expectation
　　Into their stationary vessels
　　　　And then rest in the waxing sun,
Eager for fluttering prey
　　To ride into
　　　　Death's patient spiral.

As light supplants fog
　　In the dewy mystery of
　　　　Early March,
These cloudlike tents and magic carpets
　　Ride long bent blades
　　　　With lethal precision,
Whispering softly
　　The ruthless wonder of it all.

MORNING SERMON

Squirrel in pulpit,
  Looking down on me,
    Hands braced on prone hulk
      Of rotting tree.
Your white underside—
  Pious morning vestment—
    Makes me want to
      Hear your say
And learn what
  Slowed your haste
    This day.

You contemplate
  The warm spring tease
    That lets one pause
      And feel such ease
And muse the message,
  Lost to words,
    That grounds a soaring
      Flock of birds
And plops them splashing
  In the thaw—
    The deepish, brackish, blackish muddle
      Of an unexpected puddle.

You comment on this
  Puzzling thing,
    An interlude
      Resembling spring,   ➤

And in your silent
  Sage appearing
    Tell in glances,
      Spring is nearing.
But then you halt
  Your brash surmising,
    Cancel all philosophizing,
Leap up on
  Your rotting log
    And helter skelter race and jog;
For only nature
  Calls this fling,
    This fickle, flighty
      Dance called spring;
And you must let
  The moment go,
    Since next week's outlook
      Might be snow!

MOTHER ROSE

Mother rose,
    With petals dear,
Your lifelong fragrance
    I will wear.

Your crystal freshness
    Lingers on.
Your reddest hue
    Is never gone.

From bud to bloom
    Your form has changed.
Your blossom's now
    From stem estranged.

Yet withered form
    With spirit free
Reminds me of
    What used to be.

And potpourri
    Of petals dear
Attracts, like dew,
    My treasured tear.

MY POETRY PEN

My poetry pen helps fill the space
    Between the lines of time.
A quiet minute leaves my spirit
    Free to risk a rhyme.

In measured, flowing phrases
    Words run off this point of thought;
And ideas pulling at my heart
    Look back at what they've wrought.

That trail of ink will change
    A fleeting impulse into verse.
The fluid generality
    Of mind becomes more terse.

And as my pen and paper
    Tap that vein of mind and soul,
I spill a portrait of myself
    And feel a bit more whole.

NEAR MISS

You head to work
    Before me.
You round the steep outer lane
    Of our country road,
While a young girl
    In her shiny black S.U.V.
Races toward you—
    Over the double yellow line—
Distractedly dialing
    Her cellphone,
Gabbing girl talk,
    Selecting her smoke,
        Or whatever,
And then crosses further
    Into your lane,
        Ignoring the bend in the road—
        Heading straight toward you.

Forgetting the road
    For an instant,
She leaves you in mortal danger
    As you crowd
        The steep embankment
        With no place
        To go.

➤

Her screeching last second
    Recovery, swerving right,
Saves your life, perhaps,
    And keeps her shiny vehicle—
        Her almost lethal weapon—
            Intact for yet another day;

As you and I
    Contemplate how quickly
        Life can turn
And a simple 10-minute commute
    Careen out of control
And turn your casual morning peck,
    With its simple "See you..."
Into a last kiss
    With a final farewell.

NESTING

You read my clipping
    From today's paper
Portraying two cardinals
    Valiantly defending
        Their fallen nestling.

No matter how conscientious,
    There was a point at which
        The parents could no longer
            Control the outcome
                After the babe had left
                    Their protective bounds.

The columnist reasonably extended
    This analogy
        To human fledglings
            At their different stages,
A comparison which drew
    Moisture to your eye...
        ...And then a running tear.

I had thought of our children
    At their distinctive thresholds
        Of growth and change;
And a tear had invisibly
    Infiltrated
        My thoughts, as well.

➤

That I could share
  The article with you
    And play that tear through
      To completion
Was the beauty of you,
  The beauty of parenting with you,
And the conclusive beauty
  Of you,
    Nesting with me
    In life.

NIGHT DIARY

Night dusted the earth
   With snow
And left an intimate record
   For the inquiring sun.

Dark's discreet commerce
   Had imprinted the tell-all tablet
Of road and hillside
   With hooves and paws.

Day's warming would let
   All surfaces forget
The embossed secrets of night
   And restore their confidentiality.

Darkness had inscribed a diary
   Of night's passings,
And the revealing sun
   Would soon erase all with its gaze.

NIGHT OF NO MATTER

Monday eve I bring
  The garbage out,
So Tuesday morn
  The squeaky-braked truck
    Can ingest and compress
      The leftovers of our week.

I haul the two cans
  Down to the street,
    Careful to avoid impolite scrapes
    On the night's carpet
    Of cricket sounds.

I pause at the driveway bottom
  To ingest the night,
    Press it into my feelings,
      Sip the cordial cool of September,
        Hear the pulsing chorus around me.

I stretch the time
  Standing there
    With head upraised to the stars,
      Watching an occasional smudge of cloud
      Drift over the staccato sky.

The moment is now owned
By the night,
Not by the task,
And I would unplant my feet,
Drift into the
Bespeckled dark,
And swirl out of matter
Into pure and infinite thought.

But, alas, I must first
Carry my form
Across time
To the designated pick-up point
And reverently discharge
The leftovers of one life,
Taking care not to scrape noisily
Across the carpet of life sounds
Pulsing busily
Under the night sky.

ON TOP OF THE WORLD

On top of his world,
   Atop his father's shoulders,
He scans the parking lot
   With discerning eye,
Rearranges the lofty
    Abundance of dad-hair
      Into random handfuls,
Flexes his legs and ankles
   To verify the hold
     Of parental hands,
Then rodeos back and forth
   To exult in the evening air.

My eyes could not help
   But lock on
     Their carefree stroll
       To a distant parking space
Noting that firm base,
   That secure ride,
With its remarkable show of trust
   By all such people, little or old,
     Who anchor themselves
With total acceptance
   To the existence of another.

OUTSIDE

Far outside
  Is the world of
    Buoyant bird sounds,
While I dwell on the inside
  Of thought and action
    In confined human space,
Views filtered through windows,
  Thoughts filtered through
    The gravity of objects.

For long periods,
  I go without touching
    The raw simplicity
      Of the moment,
The nothing-accomplished,
  De-scheduled,
    Sensory-enriched,
      Bare minimum
      Of being.

The structure of my mind
  Wants to forget
    Its rigid architecture,
To collapse in
  Free-floating wonder,
Lie limp
  Without regret,
Nurse life from the
  Sustaining quietude,   ➤

Disorganize thoughts
    Without fear,
Pause, where pause
    Is not indicated,
Breathe long
    Where short gasps
        Of confusion
            Are all that thrive.

Take me outside so I can
    Feel the caress of breezes,
        Surprise to simple sounds,
            Catch beauty on the fly,
                And inhale day's splendor.

PARADISE NOW

Let me understand it—
 Stuff my senses with its glare.
Let me feel the wonder
 And amazement standing there.

Let me comprehend the clear
 And overwhelming mood
That cancels any want inside
 And kindles joy renewed.

Let me burn so brightly
 At my very inner core
That I am glowing with a truth
 That doesn't long for more.

Let me brim with energy
 Sufficient to allow
That paradise is not tomorrow—
 Paradise is now.

PASSING BY

I passed my far-off past today
    And slowed to take it in.
My youth was on the practice field
    Rehearsing how to win.

So many years had slipped away—
    So long and yet a flash—
A poignant pang of yesterday
    Replayed my run and dash.

I didn't give the moment up—
    It lingered then and now.
A soothing sense of carefree calm
    Fell softly on my brow.

I hurried by my youth today—
    The players were the same;
And I was merely in the future
    Taking in their game.

PASSING MOMENT

This thing called life
   That everyone sheds
      Yet holds so dear
Is as brief
   As the cricket's song
      Or spider's weaving.

Our season, a patch of
   Winters and springs,
      Fades as fast
As the ebbing notes of night
   And the slackened fall web.

We strum our song
   And string our strands
      Against time,
Heedless of
   The craftsmen of corners
      Or minstrels of dark
As they recede
   Into the cold air
At their designated moment
   Of surrender.

➢

Stubbornly, we
    Grasp our own moment
        As long as we're able
And resist the lessons of life
    All around us,
Sure of something
    More permanent,
Hopeful of a season
    Without end.

PASSING THROUGH

Though the mountains
   Gushed spring,
This was not a day
   For stopping
      And walking.
It was, instead,
   A day for
      Passing through.

But such was the draw
   Of surging white waters
      Glancing off rocks
That I stopped my car anyway,
   Despite the shortage of day
      And the long trip ahead.

I descended to river's edge
   To touch and listen to
      The brisk run-off,
The rising chills of air
   Stroking my cheeks.

I stretched
   The allotted minute
      Into five,
Then tore myself
   From the moment's grip.

➤

This serene stopping
    While passing through
       Forgave my day
          Of its details,
Yet painfully logged
    A debt to myself
To return
    To these waters
       Some day,
Without time
    As my chaperone,

To sit,
    To observe,
       To feel again
The tranquil updrafts
    And soothing force
       Of the rushing present.

PEONY TEARS

The snow white peonies cried today,
As their bursting glory
Along our border,
Heavy from celebration,
Briefly shed their petal tears.

There was no wind to disturb them,
No cause for release,
As I passed yards away
And chanced upon
This impromptu display.

Seeing new flutter added to
Small traces of petal litter
On the near grass,
I realized this was the start
Of an end.

As I took in this moment's
Poignant message,
Another plant loosed its tears
In similar fashion,
Confirming the final days
Of this year's magnificent run.

➤

Rain or wind—or mere gravity—
Will finish the job
And litter the ground,
Much like the spillway of a waterfall
Breaks into right angles of white foam.

Green leaves will survive
This moment's glory until winter's undoing,
And next year another reunion
Of bush, bud and flower
Will spring from the earth,
Spurring a repeat of today's miracle
Of joy and farewell
Shed in tears.

PHOTO ON THE WALL

So serene and sacred
    Is this spot upon the wall.
Just a passing glance
    Affords the comfort of recall.

In a frozen instant
    Is the caring look enshrined;
Later chords of memory
    Are stirred by gaze so kind.

The spirit of a person gone
    In many ways will last;
And certain special images
    Return us to the past.

So, as we dash around our world,
    Let's harken to the call
Of peace and calm that issues from
    A photo on the wall.

PIANO MOM

No videos were there
    To log the moment;
The keys are no more livened
    By her sound.

Her pieces played by ear
    Won't grace the parlor;
No singing voices circle
    Her around.

We cannot summon songs
    In any key
Or watch her vibrant touch
    Upon the notes.

We do not feel the music
    In her soul
Or see the way enthusiasm
    Floats.

But when I hear another's
    Heartfelt playing
And sense a certain magic
    In the air

And pieces issue endlessly
    From loving,
I'm certain that her spirit
    Is still there.

PLACE OF WORK

Spiders weave into every corner,
   Stretch across doorways,
      Between objects,
Snaring those who cross
   Their air and space.

Unused desks and tables
   Are hammocked underneath
      With ancestral catacombs,
Leggy, inert sentinels
   Swaying beside alert kin.

As I bend to wipe up
   Spilled water
      From desktop coffee maker,
I view a macabre village
   Grotesquely strung
      Inside the desk opening.

I distractedly swipe away
   The newest member
      Of the clan
Unexpectedly fleeing
   The taut guy wires
      Sheared by my hand's motion
      Over the spill.

➢

Pruning a branch
  Of the local genealogy
    Distresses me slightly,
As I park the wet paper towel
  And this crumpled small fry
    In the trash
      And move on with my day.

POSSUM INTELLIGENCE

Head down, nose out,
  Legs in haste,
    As road crosses your travel.

Night leads,
  Scent drives,
    Light offends—
      Jars your concentration—
But does not slow you
  Down.

I pump my brakes
  To avoid your ashen hulk;
You glance up
  From mid-lane,
    Indignant at my bright presence,

And execute an awkward
  Turn-around and retreat,
Far too late to avoid
  My intended path,
    Had I not braked.

Night instincts
  Will prevail again
    Over the slim intelligence
      Necessary for survival;
And you will bolt forward blindly
  In search of rewards,   ➤

Only to fall prey some day
    To a less cautious driver,
With head forward, eyes locked,
    Wheels racing
        To a next destination,

Whose focused attention,
    Oblivious to the chance of you,
        Will rival your impulsiveness,
But without the excuse
    Of your primitive,
        Equally driven, feral mind.

PRESENT PERFECT

If something rare was happening,
 I didn't notice when;
For nothing caught my senses
 In the commonplace of then.

The content of the moment
 Was conventional and normal.
The phrases and exchanges
 Filled an atmosphere informal.

But something special was in progress,
 Something rare and fleeting,
Something that in later thought
 Would often bear repeating.

Unexpected moments
 Can our memories endow.
Tomorrow finds its riches in
 The commonplace of now.

PRISONERS OF LIGHT

We walked along the darkened beach
   Chasing crabs,
      Stalking their sideways motion,
         Surprising them in nighttime poses.

Beaming a clawed specter into the spotlight,
   We watched it freeze,
      Beady eyes surveying,
And then dart away
   At our first threatening motion,
      Pursued by agile flashlight,
Only again to stop in the sand's camouflage
   And find himself still
      A prisoner of light.

Then we doused our beam
   To permit his escape
      And moments later found him gone.
It was an even bet that he had either
   Back-shuffled down into the sand
      With deft claws
Or scurried off, a stop-and-go runner,
   Dashing for life
      Into the shadows.

We then walked across the beach
Into the wash of the waves
Knowing that little crabs and big crabs,
Surrounding us everywhere,
Could elude our intruding feet
In the shelter of dark.
And their discrete motions
Were as nothing
As we walked in solitary peace,
Flashlights turned off.

PROUD IN HIS SKIN

Sparely muscled bronze skin
   Meets boxers
      Three inches above
         A plunging jean waistline,
As youth struts self
   On busy state route,
      Wearing skin like a shirt,
Proud that his first work forays
   Have sprouted
      A garden of aspiring muscles
         For passersby to observe.

In the shelter of my own home,
   With an audience of
      A kind, forbearing spouse,
I may lounge in even less,
   Hopeful that my
      Youthful traces
         Haven't all succumbed
      To age
And that my rough appearance
   Has a willing beholder
      In this limited venue,

Mercifully stripped of opinions
That hubris and poor judgment
Can deal out
And the scrutiny that surely
Would have devastated me
Had I brandished
My untanned,
Softly muscled physique
On the shoulder of
A well-traveled highway.

PUBLIC BATH

Fluttering and flapping so
    And going through their paces,
Splashing in the middle of
    A parking lot oasis.

Bathing there in harmony,
    Exuberant of feather,
Occupying one small lake
    Of liquid left by weather.

This orderly confusion,
    This avian affair,
This party of immersion,
    Alternative to air.

They all exude their gusto;
    They shower and they share;
They take a bath together,
    Unabashed while playing there.

Then in this window cut in time,
    I see the moment pass;
And in a flood of energy,
    They fly away en masse.

QUICK DRAW DUO

Two short, stubby men
   Kiss their cigarettes mightily,
Punctuating their talk
   Outside the hardware store
     With shared passion
For the gray smoke
   Passing serenely
     Through their words.

Clearly both are in love
   With the fuming white stubs
     They cling to
And both admire in each other
   The rugged rituals
     Mirrored in their deep drags.

Soon they reverently pitch
   Their spent, still-lit butts
     By the curb,
As final words
   Spew small clouds
     Of farewell.

They return to high-gloss,
   Dust-free pickups
And boost themselves,
   Toddler-like,
     Into the cabs.

➤

Adult-like, and in unison,
      They welcome and fondle
Fresh unlit smokes
      Between their lips
            In familiar foreplay
Before pulling away
      From their hardware store
            Rendezvous.

They soon renew the affair
      Of experienced lips
            Embracing
                  Sensuous burning embers,
As rear view mirrors return their own
      Hard, manly glances,
And smoke trails
      Its sinewy messages
            From lonely compartments,
                  Windows ajar.

RABBIT VANITY

Your interested stare
   At the low green door
      Of my wife's car
         Amuses me.

Your break from the
   Damp uncut hillside
      With its tasty growth
To the dry, warm bluestone
   Of our driveway
      Offers no explanation.
Your unblinking eyes,
   Opposite the dark shiny door panel,
      View your image
         And the lawn and hill behind.

Do you come to admire yourself,
   Or perhaps some enigmatic other?
Are you resting and warming your feet
   While covering your rear
      Against possible predators?
Or do you clinch your gaze
   With that of an intrusive look-alike
      Competing for your
         Luscious greens?

                 ➤

You don't let on,
    Yet often I see you
        Staring two feet from
            The reflective surface,
Taking in a virtual you
    With mirrored backdrop,
As if curiosity's magnet
    And a dim understanding
        Lure you to just one more
            Meditative encounter.

RARE COURTESY

Surgical beak tears at seized duck,
Spreading its parts rudely
Over the ice.
With victim's erect head,
Feet away and attached by a sinewy cord,
Watching its own dismemberment,
The scene is a surreal comment
On the cost for one creature
Of contentment for another.

As the compact merganser
Dove into the water repeatedly
For its silvery prey
In a solitary corner of the bay,
Having ventured off
From the assembled
Canvasbacks and mallards,
It did not see nor suspect
A giant winged presence above,
An osprey soaring the drafts,
Prowling the currents
In hungry passes.

What slicing moment of opportunity
Spelled the duck's end
Is not clear,
But the results are
Indisputably
Tragic and grim,
Especially after the osprey
Lifts off from casually picked-over prey
And abandons it to crows and gulls
For their detailed study
And consumption.   ➤

In no time at all,
   Nothing at all remains
      Of the once-vibrant merganser
      (Not even the futile passes
         Of a grieving mate),
Except, perhaps,
   In subsequent times,
      These played-back memories
      And lines—
These last evidences
   Of a life:
A rare courtesy
   To a thing of nature
      Snagged unceremoniously
      Out of existence.

RAT RACE

Rat, racing across snow-brushed asphalt,
  Attracts interest of
    High-perched sentry crow,
      Who swoops down on
        Fleeing charcoal speck.

I wish the sinister shape ill
  As it bounds ludicrously
    Across the open,
      Vulnerable to crow's
        Lethal plunge.

I share the dot's panic, however,
  As it breaks into survival run
    And tries to elude
      The crow's sharp offense.

Strange relief, then, that coveting crow
  Cowers from the assault
    When snow removal apparatus
      Thunders its engine
        In mock threat.

As crow flees to secure rooftop,
  Flailing rodent scales snow bank
    And all but leaps
      To the shadow
        Of protective hedge.

➤

Nature pits creature against creature
And makes sympathetic figures of us all,
As the impulse
To survive and defend
Invades our understanding
And complicates our kind
With raw compassion.

RAW RAIN DAY

I'm up early
   In the raw rain.
House is chilly.
     Cat is timid about out.
A hint of hunger
   Says breakfast.
Cereal with bananas,
    Juice and hot coffee
      The answer.

I stay at round
   Kitchen table,
     With my pile of print,
Belly full,
   Mind hungry,
Thanking the chill morning
   For time just to sit—

Not knowing when the next
   Raw rain day
Will let my weekend
   Open up with such
     Simple, unplanned
      Space.

RAYS

Someday I will disappear
   In a poem
And the poem will disappear
   In me.

Someday the morning
   Will pass
And I will pass
   The morning.

The window admitting light
   Will close to sight.
The dwelling I inhabit
   Will be the night;

And the only rays the dark
   Will disclose
Are the wakeful lines you repeat
   While I doze—

And through the dark's
   Obscuring haze,
I'll share my fondest,
   Fairest days.

REMNANT OF SPIRIT

I'm rummaging through the past,
    And the past is impounding my thought.
I climb into letters and old situations—
    In yesterday's clutter I'm caught.

I'm awed by the way that a name
    Softly etched on the rungs of the past
Assembles the spirit of same
    Through tokens of then I've amassed.

A chest and its shoe-box keep fragments
    Of moments with life in full swing.
I'm here in the present reliving the past
    As real personalities ring.

I have to respect all the traces of then,
    Vivid chronicles touching the heart.
Tomorrow, through papers and pieces of living,
    Another may *this* moment chart.

And if they examine this shred of awareness
    In quiet reflections ahead,
My spirit will smile a warm, heartfelt greeting
    Though life and its feelings have fled.

RHODODENDRON

In first light,
    Leaves droop stiffly
        Away from buds.
Pitch-green tops
    Hug tightly closed
        Against the cold,
Wrapping center stems
    Pencil-like
        In the cutting wind.
Patient buds hide potential,
    Impassive to winter chill.

Sun inches up,
    Powdering distant hills pink,
        Glinting on night's snow,
As tendrils of warmth
    Drift slowly into shadows.

Direct rays await
    Mid-afternoon,
But leaves shed night
    And relax their tight hold
        On morning,
Letting each degree of change
    Pry their clutching shapes
        Wider open,
            Jack them a little higher.

The eventual thirty degree swing
 Over the daylight hours
  Restores their bearing,
Renews hope
 For whiffs of spring
To take away
 The sting of night
  With its snowy traces.

Readying buds,
 Stoic in winter,
  Sense season's end
   In the rising lows
    And increasing highs
And prepare to breathe
 Scent and beauty
  Into a new moment
   Unfolding.

RHYTHMS

The highermost leaves
   Hung onto the light
      As day slipped away
         And night crowded in.

And then, ever so softly,
   Day's vessel surrendered
      To night's waters;
         And last beams
            Let go their branches
               As night swallowed all.

I recall this now, days later,
   As this same leafy beacon
      Of night's arrival
         Burns ever more brightly
        On its other cheek
            To an advancing sun.

How melancholy,
   How hopeful,
      How irrevocable
         This rhythm,
That takes away
   Days, seasons, lives
      And then restores them
         In lush splendor.

RISING

At the table,
   Coffee steaming,
     Sun streaming,
Books open,
   Lines Flowing,
     Poets showing
       How alone—
Yet hardly what
   I'm sensing, feeling—
Though their words keep on
   Revealing
     Moods of mortal
     Solitude,
So well expressed,
   But then abated
     In this dwelling
When I'm fated
   One room over
     To share the knowing,
       Bear the telling,
Read the warmth
   Of your advising,
     In your now belated rising,
With your body's squeeze and press
   And touch and tender ease of showing
     Your assault on loneliness.

ROMEO AND JULIET, Sarajevo, 1993

Surviving war and hate,
   Youthful adversaries—
     Bound in love—
Struggle against
   The polarities of their
     Daily existence.

Each a fugitive
   In the other's land,
Their union contradicts
   Family and nation,
Leaving no place
   For young hearts
     To find peace.

Instead, they break and run
   From their city under siege
Heading from one hate to another
   Across that futile bridge
     Dividing enemies.

The necessity of each other
   Lets them believe
     Promises of safe passage,
But the harsh practicality of war
   Kills all hope
     In an icy hail of lead.

Through the cruel condemnation
    Of unknown sniper,
Young Serb takes his final vow
    In mute death,
        Loud enough for the world to hear;
And Muslim girl answers his vow
    With hers
As she crawls bleeding
    To his sacred, lifeless form
To bestow a last kiss,
    A last breath,
        A most holy "I do" in his arms,
As her pulse joins his
    In the matrimony
        Of eternal silence.

For six days they lay
    In conjugal closeness
        In the inert, rarified,
            In-between land
                Of war,
Uniquely alone,
    Uniquely public
        To the world,
A marriage bequeathed
    To the imaginations
        Of millions,
As a world of watchers contemplates
    What such dedication
        Would have meant
Had their love
    Been allowed to flourish
        In the unencumbered privacy
            Of each other.

RUNNING WATERS

I gazed at currents,
    Running waters
        Of the random kind.

I saw the patterns
    Weaving onward,
        Emulating mind.

I saw my life,
    Its stirring moments
        Rushing, racing by.

I saw decisions
    And solutions
        Forming on the fly.

I felt the pull
    Of chances offered,
        Choices in response,

Then saw the quiet
    Outer wake
        Of deeds attending wants

And mused at how
    This churning mix
        Of challenge, change and strife

Has a calm
    Determined fringe
        That passes for a life.

SAVE THE NON SEQUITUR

The New York Times
  Was on our kitchen table,
    Relating incidents
      Of global war and strife.
We soberly discussed
  The massacre
    Of 600 civilians
      In Liberia.

That week, the opening of
  Our backyard pool for the season
    Had left our
      Filtration system a mess,
With algae and tree debris
  Clogging our
    Diatomaceous earth filter.

Without transition or introduction,
  My thoughts wandered
    From global conflict
      To household chores.
It was in utter
  Stream of consciousness
That I said
  In casual understatement,
    "Let's change the earth today."

In spontaneous response,
  We both sighed
    And hugged tightly,
      Wishing that such could be the case.

SEA OF CHOICES

In a sea of choices,
 I cast my nets
  Over the side,
Having planned my release,
 Timed my prior moves
  As best I can.
Soon I will pull in
 My yards of mesh,
Hoping upon hope
 That in the knotted tangle
  Of experience and decision
A measure of happiness
 Will come into my boat
And that in retrospect
 I will say that my catch
  Was a good one
And that time has been friendly
 To my choices.

SETTLING IN

Heaven is a head
    Upon the pillow,
Glorious a body
    Lying prone,
Majesty a day
    Completely ended,
Miracle a moment
    All my own.

Beautiful a tired thought
    Just floating,
Patient a fatigue
    About to win,
Stunning a sweet dream
    Prepared to blossom,
Peaceful a long night
    That settles in.

SHARING SOLITUDE

The poem on my screen
    Lets me into its solitude—
        Its lonely reflection—
           As few works do.

Strange comfort to find a poet
    Willing to ask
        The anonymous reader in,
           Determined not to confound.

The thought rides with me
    On this chill November evening
As I set out down the road
    And tune in to NPR
        On the car radio,
In time to hear a peace activist
    Expound her soft logic
        To a warring world.

The car heater gradually
    Churns its warm stream
        Onto my outstretched hand;
And somehow the earlier poet
    And this current peace activist
        Are now represented
By the toasty air
    Blown into the night's
        Frigid temperature,
Rebutting what would have been
    A cold and solitary journey.

SHOSTAKOVICH'S 8TH STRING QUARTET

The eleven o'clock sun
  Drenches the table,
Lazing the steam
  From my mug upward.

Feline form stretches humanly
  From my lap
To the woven warm
  Of the placemat,
    Nudging the new-filled mug.

I press the coffee to my lips,
  Inching it empty
    Sip by sip,
While working heat-soaked fur
  In between.

I reach the lukewarm last
  And the deep down purr,
Grateful for an unhurried Saturday
  And this peaceful sharing of sun.

Shared also is the
  Music of strings,
Leading us to our own
  Private destinations
    Of purr and reflection.

➤

Peace is the meaning for me,
    Made more precious
By the composer's eloquent
    Mourning for a city's loss
        Decades earlier

And my own quiet accumulation
    Of worry for Dresdens
        Yet to be
And the possible poignant recall
    Of peaceful moments
        Such as this
            That were.

SIGNALS OF NIGHT

"Pur-*tee,* Pur-*tee,* Pur-*tee,* Pur-*tee,*"
   Sounds again and again,
As sun slips below
   Blackened green trees.

Birds ring fields and, in repeats,
   Ride the light down
      With song,
As clouds smear the sky
   Kindly
And bats—appearing, disappearing—
   Crisscross
      The marbleized blues,
         Catching a bug or two.

Audibles etch the mountains,
   As dogs toll their frustrations,
Cars and pickups
   Exude throaty noises,
Two-cycle engines chip away
   At chores,
Voices vie for attention
   In valley's heart.

Life goes on,
   As sky surrenders
      To night,
And differences wane,
   Leaving vibrant details drab
And pink-warmed slate currents
   Consuming all.

SILENT TEARS

Unkind jolt
   Stabbed at me.
You didn't, but I did,
   Perceive it that way.

That's the key—
   In the seeing
      And the feeling,
In the weighing
   And the reacting.

Tears flooded my being,
   Organically,
      Internally,
Without a trace of
   Visible salt regret,
And left me in
   Biological ruin,
      Psychological disrepair.

How often do we weep
   In the heart
      Our whale tears
And let no one
   In the world know
      But ourselves.

SNOWFLAKES

Roller coasting
　　Through the air
On giddy gusts
　　And breezes,

Dancing on
　　A breath of spirits
As the landscape
　　Freezes.

Landing in
　　The magical
Accumulating
　　White,

Contradicting
　　All the darkness
Of the hosting
　　Night.

Celebrating,
　　Congregating
On a grassy
　　Knoll,

Precious crystal
　　Waiting for
The sun to strike
　　Its soul.　　　　➤

When a most
    Amazing glint
Is what the day
    Refracts,

We're thankful for
    The evening's
Countless, miniscule
    Impacts.

SOMALI BOY, 1992

Boy with toothpick legs,
    Wilted youth starved for a future,
        Staring hollow-eyed
            At war and famine,
Seeing the hungry earth swallow all—
    First the weak
        And then, in time, the strong,
Into populous grave gardens,
    Sterile of harvest,
        Ever growing.

Your spidered gait, bowl in hand,
    Foraging for hope and mush,
        Has long since forgotten joy—
The footloose freedom
    That spends motion
        Indiscriminately,
That runs from place to place,
    Thought to thought,
        Dream to dream
            In carefree wind bursts.

Fantasies and dreams
    Elude your vanquished spirit,
Letting win
    The precocious waiting
        For life's ending—
The adult morbidity
    Of youth spent,
The bleak realization
    Of lost ripening.

➤

I try to feel
Your loss of tomorrow,
Your famished dehydration
Of spirit.
I try to dignify and separate you
From a sea of faces...
But can't.

I try to hurt for you...
And soon stretch my empathy
To breaking.
I try to apologize for
And explain
The unutterable cruelty
Of humankind...
But am forced
To look terribly inward
Without answer.

SOUTHWARD BOUND

Great blue heron heading
   To the west—
Javelin of purpose,
   Neck on breast—

Cutting through the twilight,
   Stroking air,
Shadow in the sky,
   A specter rare.

We stop in startled wonder
   As you pass—
Your mythical impressions
   We amass;

And then we note in your
   Majestic force
A change in attitude,
   A change in course.

You circle to the right
   And loop around,
Avoiding thus the river
   You have found.

You nest beyond its banks
   In nearby trees.
The dark receives you warmly
   Without breeze.

➤

When morning comes, in shallows
    You will stand,
Then soon resume your flight
    Across the land.

We envy you for leaving
    Fall behind—
To this year's killing winter
    You'll be blind.

SPIRIT AT THE CORE

A simple piece of wood or clay,
   No notes upon a score,
A sheet of paper, poem-free,
   No spirit at the core.

An art before creation,
   Humble shape without a form,
A pen before the phrases flow,
   A calm before the storm.

A striving for perfection,
   A pursuit of harmony,
A poem on the paper,
   On the score a symphony,

Out of wood a human study,
   Out of clay a flying shape.
From humans to their media,
   Assorted themes escape.

And when the marriage is complete
   And less evolves to more,
A thing becomes a work of art
   With spirit at the core.

SPITTIN' IMAGE

That awkward, empty instant
    With a country chap approaching
Stirs a mountain reflex
    From his distant vault of coaching—

A moment so spontaneous,
    When nearing cars or persons,
When judgment dims and this man's
    Smooth demeanor clearly worsens.

A slap at high society,
    A slur at fine decorum,
A nod to group behavior,
    A crudely practiced norm:

A chew, a chaw, a dip, some snuff—
    A mass of wet saliva mounts
Until his mouth is ready with
    The need to spit a juicy ounce.

He soberly regards his plight
    And quantifies his urge
Until that perfect moment comes
    When he just wants to purge.

A sloshy dark projectile
    Exits shamelessly his mouth.
The pattern could be replicated
    North or west or south.

A nearing car, approaching forms,
   A space to do his bit;
And he directs with practiced skill
   A blob of flying spit.

And in his cozy, homespun manner,
   Launched in his own way,
He spews a local version of
   A friendly, warm good day.

SPRING CELEBRATION

The peepers are ecstatic—
    The rain has launched their voices.
The drops are splashing on their heads
    And each in tune rejoices.

Spring is telling them it's time
    For bodies to arouse.
The day is late and night is not
    The proper time to drowse.

It is a time for celebration,
    Tremolo and congregation,
Appetites and urges sating,
    Musical affairs and mating.

What a frantic rite of spring—
    Their water world is everything.
Their heads and hearts are lifted high,
    And raindrops are the reason why.

SPRING PEEPERS

Silly symphony,
   Unruly chorus—
      Out of tune,
         Out of nowhere.
Squeaky night performers,
   Touting spring
      To an audience
        Of stars.
Rushing April's changes,
   Razzing winter spirits
      Still threatening frost
Who would spoil their party,
   Chill their lust.

High-pitched carnival
   Of calliope sounds
      Pouring over the night,
Celebrating and pulsing to
   Early drafts of warm air—
Premature in every way,
   But precisely on schedule
With their own
   Unscheduled,
      Impatient,
Season hurrying,
   Out-of-control,
      Helter-skelter.

STAY CALM

Be calm; avoid
    The rumble of the day.
Let peace infuse
    Your atmosphere and stay.

Affirm a breath of air
    And let it free.
Allow your petty negatives
    To flee.

Assume another image
    In the whole,
A spark amidst the galaxies
    Your role.

Let your spirit wander
    From its cell,
That center where
    Identities must dwell,

And cast your glances
    Eagerly afar,
And lean a little thought
    Upon a star,

And pull a little pleasure
    From the day,
And rush a raft of worries
    All away.

STILL FLOWING

If, in a blink,
   I am not
      And you are still,
Accept my warmth,
   Ignore the chill.

I didn't leave;
   I couldn't part.
I tapped a spring,
   Involved my heart.

I sipped a life,
   Indulged a dream,
Took off as freely
   As a stream.

And now the dream
   I chose to know
Accumulates
   A distant flow;

And moods that tumble
   From the past
Are the parts of me
   That last.

STRANDS OF LIFE

Little girl with flowing hair,
    Your mother stands and brushes you.
As with each link of loving time,
    Her warming touch still hushes you.

Despite a snarly snag or two,
    She breezes through the gold.
Her hand discovers silken thoughts
    And images to hold.

My heart discovers tenderness
    And slows the rush of life.
I feel the care effusing from
    Your mother and my wife.

I linger there in moments rare
    With glances unforgetting.
Your youthful sun is rising now;
    Your childhood is setting.

Your hands could chase the snarls away
    Without your mother's touch;
But tiny gifts that you collect
    Some day will mean so much.

And as you tuck away in time
    The magic you will miss,
We'll share with you a treasure chest
    Of moments such as this.

STROKE

Mom loved to converse,
  To communicate feelings.
She spoke out with passion
  In all of her dealings...
    But stroke took her voice away.

Her creative mind
  Had an incessant drive,
Revealing a fervor
  For being alive...
    But stroke took her voice away.

She showered her warmth;
  She bubbled with life;
She savored her calling
  As mother and wife...
    But stroke took her voice away.

She was proud, oh so proud,
  Of her husband and sons.
She eagerly talked about
  These special ones...
    But stroke took her voice away.

She was loving, so loving,
  Of her family four.
She wanted to tell them—
  She wished to say more...
    But stroke took her voice away.

➤

She drew from the children of offspring
    Such joy.
She shared wondrous moments
    With each girl and boy...
        But stroke took her voice away.

With her body's decline,
    Life beginning to wane,
She lived with discomfort,
    She wrestled with pain...
        But stroke took her voice away.

She harbored some fears—
    With questions she brimmed.
Her thoughts were quite active
    While reflexes dimmed...
        But stroke took her voice away.

She had so much more
    That she wanted to say.
She wanted to savor
    A subsequent day...
        But stroke took her voice away.

She had a small wish
    That before she did die
She could utter just one
    Final loving goodbye...
        But stroke took her voice away.

She relished this life,
    Didn't rush into death,
And all that she asked for
    Was just one more breath...
        But stroke took her breath away.

Her brow had been warm
    Leading into this day,
And her warmth would remain
    As her heat slipped away,
        Infusing our hearts as she left us that day.

She taught us the beauty
    Of life on this earth.
We learned from her going
    The joy of her birth...
        And stroke couldn't take that away.

SUMMER OF 1961

We are three brothers—
    Straddling junior and senior high school
      And college—
Availing ourselves
    Of the long summer days
      That sprawl beyond jobs and activities—
Heading to Ben Morgan's Old Ferry Dock
    On Manhasset Bay
      For an evening of water skiing.

Towels stashed, our designated oarsman
    Propels the weathered community rowboat
      To our mooring,
Where the Weasel II—
    Our 17-foot wood skiff
      Named after Dad's Weasel I
        30 years earlier—
Awaits with its brawny 75 horse Evinrude,
    Plus new mahogany deck and windshield,
      Restored after last year's devastating
        Hurricane Donna.

We start up, unmoor, return the rowboat,
    And idle quietly out of the bay,
      Sliding through moorings
        And clanking masts,

Anxious to open up our throaty V-4
   Into a widening array
      Of frothing wakes
In a race to Half Moon Beach
   Where almost two hours of non-stop skiing
      Can be pulled from the waning day.

After many runs
   With numerous punctuating wipeouts
      In the blackening waters—
         Pushing limits of energy and light—
Our exhausted crew
   Steers the agile Thompson craft
      Back home through open water,
         Shearing the waves at full throttle.

Guided by glittering shores,
   We navigate back
      To our ferry dock's bobbing rowboat
         And to a well-practiced mooring tie-up.

We are the last to return
   To the now empty dock.
Its droopy barge store—
   With its refrigerated sand worms,
      Tempting ice cream chest
         And frosty Cokes—
            Is closed for the day.

➤

We soon flood our mother's
    Welcoming kitchen
        With over-sized appetites
And grace our drop-leaf maple table
    With evening tales
        Of mighty splashes and competitive feats.
She gifts us a hearty meal,
    Garnished with her ever-bountiful spirit,
        Despite the late 9:30 hour.

So concludes this wondrous time
    Of three brothers
        Slaloming across a small cove
            On the edge of Long Island Sound
                In the intense leisure of late day,
Repeated over consecutive summers,
    Yet distilled into a single rich impression
        Slaloming warmly
            Across the waves of time.

SURVIVAL

I navigated through narrow passages
    Where survival was a matter of inches.
I looked through the chill water
    At cut edges of immovable stone.

I drifted into crisis
    As one-way walls consumed me;
And, suddenly, there was no exit
    From murderous canyons
        Intersecting my path
            Just below surface.

With annihilation just ahead,
    I had to slow, to stop, to consider
What forward motion was bringing me,
    And pinch my mortality.

Then I eased, ever so slowly, backward
    Out of this impasse,
Backed myself up from oblivion,
    And returned to a known route,
        The dull convention of survival.

There will be other canyons,
    Other treacherous thresholds
Where life will stall
    At the brink of tragedy.

➤

Once I have learned
  The route back,
   The retreat,
The reversal of fortune,
  Or misfortune,
I will feel more secure
  In life's uncharted waters,
Less afraid of myself,
  Less afraid of being.

SYMPATHETIC MOTION

As waters,
    On their downslide,
        Propel wheels,
So time,
    Running through me,
        Causes words.

Waters can wend
    Their way
        Unobstructed,
As time can
    Bypass
        Spirit's notice.

But, left in place,
    Respective heralds
        Of motion
            Do their job,
Translating flow
    Into meaning
        And marking passage
        For the rest.

THAT LIGHTNING MOMENT

That unexpected flash
　And nearby crash—
　　Who knows where—
　　　Across the air,
　　　　Upon what tree?—
Instills a fear
　Of night's potential.

The randomness
　Of it and me,
The awesome power
　Seen and heard,
The near and almost
　That's occurred,
The chance of nature's intervention,
　Merciful in its abstention,
Leaves me humbled and aware
　Of human frailties everywhere—
That raw and vivid flash of insight
　Thundering across the night.

THE ALONE

Though early yet,
    I met him
        In the alone,
Where he lay
    In still reflection,
Rushing day
    Away.

We all face
    The alone
And talk
    With ourselves
In misty moments
    When the world steps away
And leaves space
    For the mind.

Fear lurks there
    In the alone,
But we must all
    Counsel ourselves
And deal with it
    In ways we choose.

I myself,
    Sitting with him
In twilight's warmth,
    In the seclusion of
        His ninety-fifth summer,

➤

Saw that for him
    It was late in the day
And time
    For the alone to fade,
        Sleep to descend.

He saw this, too,
    As he lay there,
Like a big kid
    Tucked in
        Against time,
Pushing the alone off
    For now.

THE BRIDGE

Silent in the powder snow,
   Guided on foot by soft, shallow ruts,
We approach the rushing
   Ice-jeweled stream
     And its tranquil band of bridge.

There the road threads us into
   The quiet sanctuary
     Of a meditating deer.
We startle it
   As it startles us;
     But neither one moves.

The moment lengthens;
   And fear molds into caution
     And caution into unconcern,
As the deer bends its head
   And eyes the coursing fluid
     That separates us.

Then, what seems so natural
   And exhilarating
     In this long second
      Vanishes,
And the gentle, wild creature
   Resumes its defense,
     Abruptly darting from our day.

➤

Not at all strange
That 18 years later,
As young acquaintance
Sets off for a weekend hunt
With gun-toting chums,
I see once again
That bridge and that deer
And that brief encounter
On a quiet backroad
Of nature
And feel sad for the deer
With the briefly trusting eyes.

THE END OF NICE

Last night crickets sang their hearts out.
    Late today the warm clouds cried.
Now the evening's tepid silence
    Pokes the heartstrings deep inside.

Fall has blown rich colors off of
    Trees reluctant to disrobe.
Newly naked branches reach out
    And the blackened heavens probe.

Eerie is this bleak unfolding,
    Darkness masking beauty's plight.
All the grandeur of a fortnight
    Soon will disappear from sight.

Winds are held in brief abeyance.
    Warmth is flaunting fall's advice.
Time has stumbled; summer's haunting
    Overlooks the end of nice.

THE HILLSIDE

There's poetry on the hillside
    Inscribed upon each day,
In horses munching, grazing
    The idle hours away,

In birds on branches singing
    Their own ecstatic song,
In clouds that race across the heavens,
    Streaming thoughts along,

In sun that gazes proudly down
    On nature's fine creations,
Reflecting endless miracles
    And wondrous celebrations.

The rabbits dance their ditties;
    The crows exclaim their caws;
The winds excite the branches
    Before the breezes pause.

The cows fill in the silence
    When everything is still.
They call out to the valley
    Standing on a distant hill.

The day's familiar images
    Are sealed in memory.
Each glance upon the hillside
    Gives a glimpse of poetry.

THE IDEA OF IT ALL

God as perceived
    Ushers some until
        Their final breath
But for others
    Fades before life ends
        As brain loses
            Its remembering.

When adult turns child,
    Are earlier choices
        Of belief or non-belief
            Considered binding, erased,
Perhaps absolved
    Of eternal consequence,
Or does God remember
    Votes of faith
        Or non-faith
            As last cast?

One would hope
    The child at either end
        Of life
Is spared God's wrath—
    Or judgment—
        For opting in or out
            Of absolute certainty
Regarding the most
    Unknowable of puzzles
And that maybe geography,
    Or family, or birth,
        Or station in life
            Would allow exemptions, too. ➤

For the rest,
   It seems likely
They are going to be held
   Accountable
     For the idea of it all.

THE LIGHT (STUDYING FOR FINALS LATE AT NIGHT IN HARKNESS HALL)

As I approached the empty room,
    A light was there before me,
A sort of silent welcome
    Lest the dismal dark ignore me.

A thread of current filled
    The ceiling filament's demand.
The flow of light there flooding
    Was the act of knowing hand.

Another left the fixture going
    Conscious in the choice
That rooms are more inviting
    When they whisper someone's voice.

So when the time arrived
    To shut illumination down,
The thought of leaving darkness
    There for others cast a frown.

So as I weighed another's gesture—
    What it means to share—
I realized how such little things
    Can place a person there.

I understood how life upon a planet
    Comes and goes
And we should leave behind for all
    The light our spirit throws.

THE MEANING OF LIFE

Let me calmly focus
  On the moment
    And gaze upon the
      Meaning of my life.
Let me find some comfort
  In a smile
    And melt away
      The tensions
        And the strife.

Let me be content
  Within the quiet
    And settle for
      A scarcity of words.
Let me hear the chorus
  Of the treetops,
    The chirping of
      The insects
        And the birds.

The universe is painted
  In specifics—
    The humble things
      Are grandest
        In the whole.
I am but a moment
  In the cosmos,
    A speck of matter
      Searching
        For a role.

In the final tally
   Of the ages,
      I'll hardly leave
         A marker on my way;
But if I am alert
   To see the details,
      I'll color in
         The content
            Of today.

Each image that I seize
   Within the present
      Informs a sense
         Of fullness
            In my breast.
And if the days
   Are precious
      In the passing,
         I'll have a way of knowing
            I was blessed.

THE NATURE OF THINGS

Waiting out the long traffic light
   Where Jack's Creek Road
     Meets Route 19,
And understanding first hand
   That patience isn't always
     In the nature of things,
We watch a small parade beginning
   In the barnyard across the intersection
     As four cows emerge from
       Their evening grain and hay.

On the narrow, muddy path
   Back to their sparse winter pasture,
Lead cow slows to a near stop
   As obstructing rooster
     Claws a tardy pace,
Stooping for nonexistent
   Grain and pebbles,
     Cockily blocking the procession.

Impatient following cow
   Nudges first cow
     Out of the way
And stampedes through
   Arrogant rooster,
Launching it in the air
   With a blunt nose
     Under tail feathers,
Thus getting back to
   The serious business
     Of early evening,
Which isn't indulging
   A rooster with attitude,

As we have indulged
   This long red light
      With rapt attention
To an amusing,
   Well-timed showing
      Of the nature of things—
Curtain finally closing
   As light turns green
      And we hurry on our way.

THE NEAT ROOM

The neat room
    Wore "empty"
        All over it.
The scattered clothes
    That marked it "full"
        Were cleaned, folded,
            Packed, shipped,
                Or stored.

The crowd of possessions
    And papers
        That once clamored
            "I am here"
Had been put away,
    Thrown away,
        Or taken away
To where he is now,
    In a little college town
        In the mountains.

The clean carpet,
    The made bed,
        The absent discards of laundry
Echoed a new life beginning,
    A life which would soon
        Find its own
            Meaningful clutter
And supply a new space,
    A new circle,
        With the fullness and goodwill
            That he carries like a backpack
                Each step of the way.

Meanwhile, this empty room
Did not shout "loss"
At every glance.
The shared excitement
Bonding a family together
Made the empty room
A symbol of discovery,
Not separation.

The awaited emotions faltered,
Because the connection
To dreams unfolding
Was stronger than
Any short-sighted
Notion of grief.

The neat room
Was merely another thing
Stored for tomorrow,
Another garment
Ready to keep the cold out
And love in.

THE REPRIEVE

The moment's reprieve—
    All our terminal fears
Of his body's decline
    Due to onset of years

Are proven untrue,
    For the moment at least.
With grief in abeyance,
    No tears are released.

I wrestle my sadness
    Back into its cage.
I turn back the plot
    From its ultimate page.

I let it continue
    Without my intrusion;
Time will determine
    This story's conclusion.

I wait and pretend
    That I'm really not waiting,
Yet fears that assail me
    Are scarcely abating.

I watch as our magical
    Moments extend,
Relieved that the time
    Isn't ripe for an end.

THE STREAM

The stream is there beside the house,
    A sign for generations.
It marks for us the flow of life
    With timeless orchestrations.

The stream calls out through ages past
    To ages yet ahead.
It draws us to observe its pulse
    On banks to which we're led.

It is the same inviting force,
    The surging rush of power,
That shared with other witnesses
    Its strength in former hour.

It is the brisk appealing sound
    That called to those before.
It is the vital message
    That will sing to countless more.

Its passing tune to sun and moon,
    To every dusk and dawn,
Will tell the truth of waters past
    To others later on.

THE WATCHMAN

His small hillside farm
    Stretches across a bend
    In the road.

From the grassy slope
    Near his house,
        With elbows braced on knees,
He seems transfixed on
    The occasional passing car.

I think to wave
    As I slow through the turn,
But his transcending downhill stare
    Urges my look forward,
        Not wanting to violate
          His sanctuary.

I see him in this pose
    Several times
        As the warm season unfolds
And realize that
    While facing the road
        He also faces an evolving
        And substantial
          Plot of vegetables.

Truth is, he is most likely not
    Watching the cars go by;
        He is watching his
          Vegetables grow,
As I have also been doing
    Day by day.

In time, navigating my car
    Through the early morning haze,
I am more likely to see him
    Seated with his wife
        At an old redwood table
Proudly studying beans or squash
    Or cucumbers.

Now the corn stands tall
    With darkening tassels.

In the coming days,
    It won't surprise me
        To see the old farmer,
            Elbows on knees,
Reading the stalks
    From the hillside,
Waiting until that
    Very last moment
        When green golden ears
            Spill over his redwood table
And he and his wife glory in
    The creation and harvest
        They so love.

I now better understand
    That steady stare
        Down the hillside,
            That patience with time,
That left me so curious
    Earlier in the season.

THE WATCHMAN: EARLY HARVEST

I didn't know the old couple,
But they farmed together
On the fertile river land
Across the highway
From their house.

Their machines and labor
Transformed the lower fields
Each year
Into productive rows
Of corn, squash,
And whatever else.

I saw them last year
Sorting some of the season's
Vegetables
On the redwood table
By the road.

I saw him building
The new steel shed
In front of the old
For his tractor
And farm implements.

Then, instead of this year's
Lush mid-season indicators
Of shared effort
I saw the "Slow, Funeral" sign
Planted on the highway shoulder
In both directions.

I saw the floral wreath
    Hanging from the window
    Of their home.
I saw a few more cars
    Parked on their grass
    Than ever before.

I saw the weeds
    Dominating their fertile soils
    This growing season;
And I saw his obituary
    In the weekly paper,
Humbly excusing
    The only complete rest
These fields, and he,
    Had known
        In a pile of years.

THE WORD OF THE DAY

On our evening walk
    Up the mountain road,
We study butterflies and flowers,
    Plentiful masterpieces
        Of a warm summer day.

Covering every fertile surface,
    Blues, pinks, lavenders and yellows
        Decorate undulating greens
            Of untamed meadow,
Garnish untrimmed shoulders
    And embankments of the road.

Swallowtails flutter and probe
    Nectar secrets of fields
        And roadside floral clusters,
Swooping at us head-on
    With near collisions,
Unaccustomed to onlookers
    Blocking their exuberant chaos
        Of exploration.

The half-hour up
    And half-hour down—
Escorting the sun lower,
    Shadows longer—
Fill us with nature's sweetener,
    God's bounty,
As we slowly return to
    The deliberate world
        Of daily life.

During the descent,
Friends stop their car briefly
To greet us
On the way to town,
As they head to their church's
Mid-week worship and study
To discuss and better understand
God's written words.

We smile in appreciation,
Inwardly reviewing
The sacred words
Spoken to us in images
Drawn on a tablet
Of simple meadows
In wondrous flourishes
Of swallowtail script.

THREE COUNTRY GENTS

Three heads on upright shoulders,
    Unavoidably close
In the cab of an old
    Blue and rust Dodge Ram pickup

Saunter slowly ahead of me
    Contemplating a right turn,
Which, when executed, forces hardly a lean
    From the trio.

Old weathered heads,
    Two with baseball caps,
One with gray hair
    Struggling to cover the crown,

Neatly dressed wooden
    Scarecrows, facing forward,
Stiff and dutiful in intent,
    Precisely spaced, untouching,

Headed, perhaps, for Hardee's
    And a biscuits and gravy breakfast
Topped with coffee and a
    Splash of cream

And a bit of terse talk
    Overflowing into dry conversation,
Amusing enough to juice the eyes
    With an occasional smile.

The table talk will outlive
    The tidbits of local fare
And the coffee will be nursed
    Until its steam cools

And the three will then
    Adjourn, unhurried,
Back to their pickup
    To assemble in the cab,

Country gents, upright and stiff,
    Precisely spaced
And necessarily close
    On the firm spring support

And sparse comfort
    Of an old pickup seat,
Heading without haste back
    To where they came from.

TIMES THAT SHOULDN'T END

Times that touch emotions
    Are the flowers life may send;
And moments all too precious
    Are the times that shouldn't end.

But all the bouquets of a life
    Are never meant to last;
And while we try to nurture them,
    They slip into the past.

As a fleeting moment fills with change
    And shadows grow,
We must deal with realizations
    Sorrowful to know.

And as the day begins to ebb
    And flowers start to bend,
A moment that has touched our heart
    Appears about to end.

Just one thing retains for us
    The colors that have shined:
The fertile field of memory—
    The flowers of the mind.

TO SOAR NO MORE

You stand where others
　　Preened and sunned
　　　　On dock attached to shore;
And now that they have
　　Flown away,
　　　　You're apt to soar no more.

With wounded leg
　　And broken wing,
　　　　You stand alert and still.
Your mind could carry
　　You aloft,
　　　　If all it took were will.

But now you're captive
　　To the land,
　　　　Consigned to shore and sea.
You cannot sail among
　　The wings of others
　　　　Flying free.

You'll hear the distant wingbeats
　　And the gabble
　　　　Of the flock
And see them fade
　　Into the haze
　　　　As rowdy sea gulls mock.

➤

Raw nature will not
    Pamper you
        As time absorbs the seasons.
Advancing cold
    Erodes a life
        And drains a will of reasons.

And as you watch
    The other geese
        In drafts above the shore,
Your heart will pound
    The piercing truth
        That you may soar no more.

TODDLER TALK

"Be careful" and "do it carefully"
Were words our two-year-old
Seemed to grasp
When falls and scraped knees,
Or spilt juice,
Were a possibility
And slow, deliberate action
Was our parental wish.

It came as a pleasant surprise one day
When the youngster's
Expanding vocabulary
Redefined for us
The slow, vertical dusting of snow
In our backyard,
Free of disturbing wind.

He thoughtfully observed
That the snow
Was falling "carefully."

If our toddler had heard
Words of caution to excess,
It still did not take away
The delightful poetry
Of the moment
In which he cast the delicate snowfall
Observed through our back window
In such a loving light.

TOY VILLAGE

Toy houses dot
Distant hills and valleys,
Hugging ribboned country roads,
As toy cars, trucks
And school buses pass by.

Our house peers quaintly
Across the valley,
Its details scaled down
To distant eyes,
Our cars, likewise, turned to
Miniature play things.

Hard to imagine what drives
And occupies
Car or dwelling
From a remote viewpoint.

Thus it is with distance,
The perspective of separation:
We can only invest
Far away persons,
Structures or things
With imaginary traits.

If leaps across valleys
    Can be challenging
        To the understanding,
One can imagine how difficult
    Those across regions, nations
        And continents can be,
Given those distant props
    Of the imagination,
The toys that fuel—
    Or at times even savage—
        Our compassion.

TRACKING THE SOURCE

Water slips down the age lines
   Of the mountain,
Joining and re-joining
   In ever-widening flows.

The earth's deep down pressures
   And replenishing rains
Drive these lithe, spirited messengers
   To far-off confluence
In rivers, lakes and oceans
   For reunion and re-dispersal.

As we climb the mountain,
   We track origins,
     Get to the source of things,
Dividing and subdividing
   Our understanding
Until we reach
   The most distant spring
     Exiting earth.

As with all secrets,
   We track our clues
     As far as we can
Along the tributaries
   Of our knowledge

Until our understanding
Disappears into the heart
Of something much larger
And we have only the nearest spring
Effusing earth's endless humors
To address our imaginings.

TRAIN WHISTLE

Rushing through the night,
  Last diesel to Northport
    Punctuates its journey
      With long whistle bursts
        At each crossing.

Flashing gates
  Salute passage,
    Holding occasional cars
      At attention.

Wholesome clatter
  Melds with the night,
    Meets our expectations
      For purposeful, routine,
        Not-too-distant noise,
Settles us further
  Into a reassuring structure
    Of evening thoughts
      And observations,
Nudging our last
  Insecurities
    Out of the way.

Manmade resonances
　　Of rail
　　　And the last
　　　　Rolling stock
　　　　　Of commuters,
Stretching their day
　　Past ours,
Fulfill night's final adieu
　　The way a family member
　　　Arrives late
　　　　After a day
　　　　　Of strenuous doing.

TRANSITION

The morning sky
　Looks down through
　　The thinning forest
　　　To our bedroom door,
As a deer threads
　The matchstick hillside,
　　Bowing to fragile
　　　Shoots and greens.

Each gasp of wind
　Stirs ruddy leaves
　　In mock rainfall,
As the brawny silhouette
　Crosses our view.

This somber shadow spirit,
　Bereft of summer's
　　Generous cover,
Can no longer hide
　In hill's abundance
And must spend
　The banked flesh
　　Of warmer days
　　　On the colder,

As I, too, must
　Lean my own
　　Expectations
In the thinning forest
　Of a harsher season
　　About to begin.

TREES IN MOTION

The trees and the branches are waving
    Their vigorous answer to wind.
They motion in every direction
    With energy undisciplined.

These gusts are more active than breezes
    That fondle and fuss about limbs.
They follow their urges and impulses
    And act out their notions and whims.

The little trees shimmy excitedly;
    The larger ones firmly respond,
So that every branch tipping and leaning
    Has the sweep of a grand magic wand.

The forest delivers the message
    Of each new arrival of air.
In roars, the trees are revealing
    The ways in which they are aware.

They're always preparing and flexing,
    So every new challenge they bear;
For the wind can be mellow or merciless,
    Its attitude callous or fair.

And the days and the nights are rehearsals
    For all that the season can send,
And sessions of tossing and turning
    Are the serious side of pretend.

TRIBUTE TO SNOW

Descending the slick road
    In bitter cold,
I glance through the sparse border of trees
    At the small, tidy graveyard,
Brushed with snow,
    Bursting with flowers.

The granite markers
    And colorful plastic tributes
Clamor for spring,
    When the plush green sod
Will again make the picture
    Whole.

Right now, the flowers,
    Lifeless and out of time,
Speak the blunt truth,
    That spring, in time,
Will soften with its
    Compensating grandeur.

I don't know which is better—
    The bitter frost of winter
With its colorful truth-telling
    Bouquets
Or the mitigating abundance
    Of spring
With its poignant suggestion
    That the flowers are real.

TWO BRANCHES OF ONE SPIRIT

Two branches of one spirit,
 Two brooks within one wood,
Rush down from two directions
 And unify for good.

The eons etch a pattern
 Upon the hills and slopes.
The rains then read the surfaces
 Of independent hopes.

The waters tumble to their goal,
 A confluence ordained,
A miracle of meeting,
 A wonder unexplained.

They tumble now together—
 They form a single flow.
Their dreams and their desires join—
 Their flooding passions grow.

Two branches of one spirit
 Now rush along as one;
And time will sing their special song
 Of sharing till it's done.

TWO KITES

Two overhead kites
 Coasting the high breeze
  With enormous tails
  Shimmering
   In full extension
Shadow our play
 As we weave our moves and passes
  Over the fabric
  Of our field
   Of action.

When one overseer is withdrawn,
 Pulled back to earth,
  Another supplants it,
A motionless construct
 Of extended wings
  Coasting the relentless currents.

I am alone in pointing out
 Its majestic realism
  Hovering intimately alongside
   The remaining bark-papered craft;
And I have difficulty
 Returning my attention
  To the earthbound
   Elements of our play.

Then, on one upward glance,
I exclaim as I watch
This grand winged specter
Unexpectedly release
Its grip on the air
And drift gracefully
Downwind,
Suddenly upstaging the kite
Which was the object
Of its own
Intense scrutiny,

And so relaying to us
A large hawk's
Considered opinion
That the clumsy tailed object
Made of paper and sticks,
Cowering on modest tether,
Would not likely heave anchor
And pose any threat
To its ample avian domain
Whatsoever.

UNCHAINED MELODY

Two chainsaws harmonize
    On a hillside,
        Cutting to the core
        Of things
            As they now stand.

They buzz through bark,
    Revving up and revving down
        As the grain demands,
            Vanquishing years of growth
            And tall-reaching forest
Into horizontal lengths and logs,
    Bare of branches,
        Sprawled in a chaos
        Of battlefield litter.

Energies driving this raucous
    A cappella of saws—
Starting and stopping,
    Again and again—
        End in sweaty exhaustion,
Leaving only stillness—
    Awesome emptiness—
        For the imaginations
        Of distant listeners
Who noticed the battling melodies
    From afar
        And know their cost,
Surely failing to catch the exultation
    Of a day's work completed
        And nestlings of the human kind
        Provided for,
After the assault on nestlings
    Of another kind,
        Once perched so high.

UNSUNG HERO

How you work your quiet magic
   Is a wonder to behold.
How you find a way of helping
   Is a story to be told.

How you choose to get involved
   In ways that stretch imagination,
How you give the world a heart
   And seek to chase away frustration,

How you use your intuition
   As a basis for concern,
How your actions are the reason
   For the high respect you earn,

How you work behind the scenes
   And ask no credit for your deeds,
How your radar always knows
   When those around you have great needs,

Speaks about your gift of kindness,
   Tells about the role you fill,
As a special unsung hero
   Sharing your unselfish skill.

VIRTUAL REALITY

Long-legged spider,
  Tangling our entryway
   With filaments
    By night,
Disturbed by our
  Daily openings
   Which tear your weavings
    Asunder,
Scare me away this time—
  Intimidate me
   With your wild shaking,
    Your brazen acrobatics.

Pivot your body
  Back and forth
   Lightning fast
    With elastic tethers.
Impress me with your
  Blurred enormity,
   Your sudden growth.
Hurry up and finish
  Your fearsome show
   Of defiance,
So I can resume
  My activities
Without, for the moment, entering
  Your well-defended space.

We humans emerge from our own night,
Shaking words and grandiosities
At the fates
From earthly tether,
Thinking our enlarged presence
Will chase away
Huge unknowns
That disturb us
And rock our anchors
Every waking day.

Like the spider,
Our vigorous shaking
Disguises our avoidance
Of the obvious
And lets us hide in
The blurred, self-inflating reality
Of our own limitations.

WAITING

Petite squatter,
    Your tiny web home
        Connects wicker basket bottom
To wood molding
    In the dark bathroom corner.

I tolerate,
    Almost count on,
        Your presence each day,
Nimbly centered in your
    Three inch netting,
Awaiting the prey
    My eyes can't see,
But yours must
    Surely anticipate.

I can only imagine the alertness
    Fueling your
Static vigilance
    As you survey your minute realm.

A life so centered
    Perplexes my humanity
As I leave you behind
    In your dark world,
Magnifying the microscopic,
    Shoring up your geometry
In the untethered world
    Around you,
As I depart
    To shore up my own.

WARM OCTOBER NIGHT

The night was still, October warm,
    With summer insects sleeping.
A single cricket was the only
    Watch the night was keeping.

This evening without wind
    A lonely distant train was heard.
A solitary peace urged us
    To quiet breath and word.

We pressed our senses to the night,
    Which hardly spoke at all.
Our listening was punctuated
    By an acorn's fall.

The soloist of night alone
    Engaged our rapt attention.
The chill of fall had long dismissed
    Night's chattering convention.

The cricket chirped in mourning
    Now his orchestra was gone.
He played his plaintive piece for us
    Until approaching dawn.

We slept with windows open
    Out of courtesy for one
Who kept his patient vigil
    Though his summer's theme was done.

WE'RE WITH YOU ALL THE WAY

We're with you all the way, my dear;
    We've come to say goodbye.
We're following behind you, dear,
    Your trip to sanctify.

It's been a lengthy journey—
    Still our journey isn't through.
We're with you all the way, my dear.
    Soon we'll be there with you.

Your spirit free now dwells in me
    And all of those you love.
The air we breathe is sacred now
    With beauty from above.

You led us through our life 'til now
    As wife and mother, too.
You've so enriched us with your gift
    Your life will ne'er be through.

You gave us life in many ways—
    Through love you were our birth.
You gave us all the eyes to see
    The wondrous things on earth.

Until our focus fades into
    The vastness you now see,
We'll be your living eyes
    And living heart until we're free.

Our time of separation
    With such sadness fills our day;
Yet your beauty fills our memories—
    We're with you all the way.

WHEN I WRITE NO MORE

When I write these words no more
    And all of life has spilled from me
And all the essence of my world
    Has poured into my poetry,

Allow a moment, now and then,
    To view with me this narrow space—
Examine every detail there,
    Reflect upon the commonplace.

If you share with me the wonder,
    Find in nature your reward,
Keep your interest in the meager,
    You will never end up bored.

Every stone that you turn over,
    Every leaf a tree sets fly,
Every sky that fills with glory,
    Every season passing by,

Tells of precious moments fleeing,
    Tells of tides that wash away,
Tells of times that we should notice,
    Tells of moods that color day.

When my phrases flow no longer,
   When this poet breathes no more,
When this heart is still and silent,
   Let a breeze pass through your door.

Watch a bird exult in flying,
   See a cloud arrive and pass,
Track a seed upon its journey,
   Idle barefoot on the grass.

There is always more to capture;
   There is always much to see.
When my senses soar no longer,
   Take a little walk with me.

WHEN TIME STANDS STILL

The crystalline perfection
Of a moment locked in time
Distills its true reflection
Into memory sublime.

A day when progress halted
And time, it seemed, stood still,
We sipped of pure simplicity
And couldn't get our fill.

We focused on the plainer truths;
We saw with clearer eyes;
We shunned the clutter in our lives
And thus became more wise.

Life has certain jewels
That are timeless and are rare.
They captivate us humbly
In a breath of pure spring air.

WHITE BUTTERFLIES

Off you go,
  Lofting so,
Meeting and
  Dividing.

Find the flow—
  Ripe you go—
Tumbling,
  Confiding.

Independent,
  Drifting off,
Seeming so
  Detached,

You return
  In raw excitement,
Flying closely
  Matched.

All your motions
  And emotions
My emotions
  Stab.

Empty of all
  Color,
You are anything
  But drab.

WHITE LIE

Fog consumes morning;
Mist crowds out details;
Clouds laze on land.

Sun struggles for recognition;
Sky waits patiently;
Trees hold onto gray.

Day sounds begin;
Fog, confusing time,
Forces clocks to lie.

Sun, pestering fog,
Dissolves the nebulous white,
Wins back day.

WHO ARE YOU?

"Who are *you*?" she asked her spouse
    Of more than 60 years.
Before, he was the world to her,
    Yet time dissolved her tears.

She didn't know just who *she* was
    Or what had slipped away.
She couldn't pull from memory
    The things she'd like to say.

Her only conversation
    Was to ask what day or season.
Her intellect and fast response
    Were gone with no clear reason.

She had a winning smile
    But at times a vacant stare.
She was lost and floating by
    Without a single care.

There was a time of autumn leaves,
    But this was winter's tune.
We all could not forget how much
    It meant when it was June.

WINDSTORM

Oak trees thrash about
   Like wind-swept wheat.
Clouds splash their contents
   Into cross drafts,
Fracturing droplets
   Into heavy mist.

Crickets blast their songs
   Confidently over noisy gusts,
Determined to use every minute
   Of the waning season.

The sky collects all of night's
   Available light
In frothing pink and yellow
   Radiance.

Acorns clunk noisily
   On cars and gutters.
Screens whistle weakly
   To accelerating winds.
Branches hyperextend
   In agonied cracks.

Night is alive
With the soft fury
Of a hurricane downgraded
To a tropical storm.

Life is alive
With the sleeplessness
Of a full-featured night
Of rare and ominous beauty.

WINTER BREATH

Winter let out
    Its first snowy breath
        This morning
And then inhaled it
    Right back
        Before earth
            Could notice.

Its gentle
    Understatement
        Caught us unawares,
And we scarcely read
    The meaning of
        The day's quiet passing.

Yet winter's message
    Is delivered irrevocably
        To those near;
So that once
    Summer and fall
        Let go of the mind,
Nothing is quite
    The same
        Thereafter.

How long and hard
    This barren season repels
    The civility of spring
Parallels the way grief
    In its strong renunciation
    Of solace
Spends itself out
    Before finding
        The lengthening days
        Of tomorrow,
The strengthening suns
    Of hope.

Snow fell today
    For the first time
And quietly reminded us
    That abundance
        Will have to await
        Its turn
While eddies of doubt
    Briskly rule
        The negative winds
        Of now.

WITHOUT A SOUND

The woods are folded up tonight,
  The insect rhythms
    And occasional rustles
      Gone.
The fireflies are doused,
  The dogs across the valley
    Mute;
The birds lie still in nests
  Free of flutters and chirps.

Everything that was
  Or is to be
Surrounds this unnatural,
  Yet wholly natural,
    Quiet.

In the usual diversity of dark,
  Silence stands out,
As my ears drill the night
  For traces of anything;
And patience reveals
  But the broken fall
    Of a black walnut
      Caroming to the forest floor.

The pact of silence
   Remains,
      As I drift away
         On slumber's ocean current,
Hoping my sometimes audible inhales
      Don't mar the moonlit night
         And its tranquil play
            Of beams and shadows.

WOODPECKER

Nature's little
    Wake-up call—
I know your gentle
    Clamor.
Why today
    Did you decide
To mock a mean
    Jackhammer?

In the distant
    Trees you were
A welcome noise
    Of morning.
Now you've shed
    Your normal role—
My gutter
    You're adorning!

What has been
    A tasteful
Rat-tat-tat,
    A far off din,
Now becomes
    A Gatling gaffe,
A feather-headed
    Sin.

When you wish
        To amplify,
List oak among
        Your urges.
But don't be one
        Of nature's louder
Heavy metal
        Scourges.

YELLOW PANSY

There's a yellow pansy
    In the planter by the door.
Its cheerful spot of color
    Isn't easy to ignore.

Its battle for survival
    Is a miracle to tell.
By night it shrivels up
    And bows its face to its lapel.

The temperatures keep dropping—
    Though the days rebound a bit—
And on our deck the single yellow
    Pansy is a hit.

No other flower prospers
    Through the early winter's frost.
No other plant has failed to pay
    The season's heavy cost.

But after cold and wind by night
    Have left this sprite dejected,
The sun restores it back again,
    Its spirit resurrected.

Courageously the passage
   Of the season it ignores;
But it can't hold this bright appearance
   Everyone adores.

And in some morning, time will win—
   A mist will cloud our eyes;
And we will mourn the passing of
   This solitary prize.

YOSHINO CHERRY

Spring litter,
　　After-party confetti,
　　　　Scene of celebration,
Tossed on grass,
　　Hugging curb,
　　　　Spilt across asphalt—
　　　　　　Much more coming.

Afternoon lull,
　　Day is dry,
　　　　Sun concentrates,
　　　　Wind rests.
White polka dots,
　　Slipping grip
　　　　Yet holding on,
Till a petty gust
　　Or gentle spritz
　　　　Sets a few loose
　　　　　　In a tumbling flutter
　　　　　　Of light.

What if an afternoon shower
　　Blows into town,
　　　　Base drums blaring,
Calling the party,
　　Canceling plans,
　　　　Stripping sunburst wardrobe
　　　　　　To near-naked green?

The consequence of a confused
85 degree March day
With a busted party
Surely would be
Heaps of leaden white drops
Scattered all over—
Sticky new compost
With nowhere to go...

Skies therefore must not unload,
Ruin things,
Route the festivities.

Implore the light-hearted day to drag on,
Beg the elements to be kind,
And let the party continue!

YOUTH

Youth rides with us
    Until we're done.
It never notes
    The setting sun.

It only minds
    The way we see
A leaf upon
    November's tree.

If life is measured
    In the pall
Of this poor leaf
    About to fall,

Then youth and its
    Eternal dawn
Through this concern
    Is nearly gone.

But if that rusty
    Leaf we see
Still decorates
    This autumn tree,

Then youth stays with us
    Till the end
Though wind and storm
    These branches bend.

ZEPHYR

The gusting breeze
    Of you came through
And paused for
    Just a while.

Time couldn't snare
    Your rush through air;
Time couldn't keep
    Your smile.

The journey loomed;
    The wind resumed
And led you
    Into sky.

The noble wait
    In time for fate
Then let you
    Hurry by.

I weep because
    Our own brief pause
Receives the draft
    Of you,

Reminding us
    Each wind that stops
Will soon be
    Passing through.

Some of the poems in this book have been selected from previously published works by the author. They appear on pages in this book as follows:

FEELINGS (1987): Poems on pages 30, 121, 158, 199, 332, 348

LOVE POEMS (1990): Poem on page 332

BELIEVE IN YOURSELF (1998): Poems on pages 17, 20, 42, 59, 90, 127, 132, 138, 147, 177, 180, 181, 200, 206, 209, 212, 215, 225, 241, 244, 248, 250, 251, 268, 269, 277, 279, 289, 290, 297, 306, 332, 338, 348

TIME CRIES (2011): Poems on pages 277, 338

POEMS TO CARRY WITH YOU ON LIFE'S JOURNEY (2012): Poems on pages 147, 225, 250, 268

POEMS FOR THE ONE I LOVE (2013): Poems on pages 60, 117, 249, 332

Bruce B. Wilmer lives in the Blue Ridge Mountains of western North Carolina. He is married and has two grown children. His poetry books and products have been enjoyed by a worldwide audience of millions for over 40 years.